Boris's Bus

The book team would like to thank (in alphabetical order) Johor Ali, Ian Craig, Leon Daniels, David Ellis, Kevin Ellis, Katy Harris, Sir Peter Hendy, Hilton Holloway, Pieter Lesage, Jamie Martin, Alan Millar, Simon Paterson, Alan Ponsford, Marek Reichman, Ann Reinking, Ian Rivett, Malcolm Robson, Antony Roskoss, David Stewart, Toby Tinsley, Peter Waller and those who assisted anonymously. Thanks also of course go to Boris Johnson, without whom the bus and therefore this book would not exist.

Designed by James Whiting and Lucy Frontani

First published 2013

Second and enlarged edition 2015

Published by Capital Transport Publishing Ltd

www.capitaltransport.com

Printed by Parksons Graphics

Boris's Bus

Capital Transport

John Aldridge
Gavin Booth
Stewart J Brown
Hilton Holloway
Keith McGillivray
Alan Millar
Matt Prior
James Whiting
Christian Wolmar

"CAN SOMEONE GET ME A TICKET?!"
THE BOOK OF MORMON
LONDON UNITED
Hammersmith 9
LTZ 1076

BORIS JOHNSON'S PLEDGE

JAMES WHITING

While speaking in September 2007 about the following May's London mayoral elections, Boris Johnson announced that if selected as Conservative party candidate and subsequently elected, he would hold a competition to design a 'new Routemaster' and also replace the bendy buses that had been introduced during the time Ken Livingstone was mayor. The bendy buses were unpopular with motorists and cyclists, while Routemasters had been reduced to operating on two special 'heritage' routes since last running in normal passenger service in December 2005.

In his 2008 manifesto, Johnson included a pledge to introduce what he called a '21st Century Routemaster' to London's streets, saying that he wanted to 'once again give London an iconic bus' that Londoners could be proud of. He confirmed he would commission a competition 'for the world's best designers and engineers to design a brand-new Routemaster that is fully compliant with EU legislation, has disabled access and is run on green fuel'. He coupled this with a promise that when routes operated by bendy buses came up for contract renewal, he would specify that different types of bus would have to be used.

Boris's bus promises became a focus of hot debate in the lead up to the mayoral election. Most of the argument was around the cost of his plans. Various figures were quoted, including one of £112m per annum by Transport for London in March 2008 that Boris interpreted, rightly or wrongly, as an attack on his campaign. He was however largely dependent on TfL for cost estimates and conceded the following month that £100m was about right.

The official figures being quoted for the project comprised the cost of conductors and additional buses and drivers to make up the passenger capacity lost by replacing high-capacity bendy buses with double-deck buses. At the time that Boris was publicising his intention of replacing the bendy buses, there were 399 of these in London. To maintain the passenger capacity it was estimated that 620 of any new double-decker would be needed. The estimate of additional costs of £112m per year was made up of 1,736 conductors at £28,000 each per year, 651 extra drivers at £35,000 (both figures including employer's National Insurance and pensions) and £40m a year for the new buses.

In the election, Boris was standing against Labour's Ken Livingstone, who had been mayor since 2000 (when he stood as an independent) and who had been the first person to hold the position. When the election results were announced, Boris Johnson had overtaken Ken's lead in early opinion polls and was declared the winner, having received 53.18% of the final votes compared with 46.82% for Ken. Many saw transport as one of the main contributors to Boris's victory – including his bus pledges, a crackdown on illegal minicabs and his promise to reverse an unpopular extension of the congestion charge into inner west London that Ken Livingstone had introduced.

At the launch of his 2008 London mayoral election campaign, Boris Johnson holds a model Routemaster to publicise his plan for a 21st century version.

With a majority of around 140,000, Boris became mayor and in consequence what might have been just a dream for a new bus for London became a reality. Whether that reality would extend to more than the eight prototype buses that were built depended on the result of the following election, in 2012, when Boris once again stood against Ken. Boris of course pledged to build a fleet of the new buses if re-elected; Ken had other ideas. Boris had become a popular mayor, generating much affection by being a politician who was quite often politically incorrect and projecting an image of not taking himself too seriously. To some extent Ken had achieved popularity for the same qualities. However, it seems possible that the popular pledge on the 'new Routemaster' swung it for Boris, who won the 2012 contest, albeit with a reduced majority of 62,500. Outside London, new jobs in the bus industry depended on that result, leading to the unusual occurrence of celebrations across the Irish Sea around the result of a London mayoral election.

So, because of its origins, the New Bus for London, Boris Bus, New Routemaster, Borismaster or whatever you want to call it, became a very political issue and whether or not someone was in favour of the bus was very often determined by whether or not they were in favour of Boris. On the question of whether the bus represents good value for money, opinions are still sharply divided. Alongside considered and informed opinions, there has been much strongly biased comment.

Johnson on the platform of a Routemaster with campaign message.

THE DESIGN COMPETITION

CHRISTIAN WOLMAR

The promise of a New Bus for London was prompted by nostalgia and a desire to keep alive the idea of the iconic Routemaster. This reverence for the Routemaster rather ignored its real history. When it was first introduced, the Routemaster was notoriously unreliable, with many breakdowns and with automatic gearboxes that gave a jerky ride. These problems took some time to overcome before the Routemaster came to be regarded as a reliable bus with a classic design. Apart from a couple of heritage routes, the 9 and the 15, the last Routemasters in London had run in December 2005. Ken Livingstone, who first became mayor in 2000, had originally supported retaining the buses, which were much loved by Londoners and tourists alike, but realised that with the extensive use of Oyster cards, the expense of keeping the old buses going and, crucially, the lack of access for disabled passengers and buggies, they should be phased out.

Then politics entered into the story. In September 2007, the Conservative mayoral candidate, Boris Johnson, trailing in the polls at the time, announced that he would support a competition for a new bus for London based on Routemaster principles, most notably an open platform at the back. This attracted considerable attention, not all of which was positive. *Autocar* magazine's Hilton Holloway recalls:

'The strength of the condemnations of Johnson's policy of commissioning a new bus spurred me into action to help. One evening in October 2007 I was lamenting at the *Autocar* office what I saw as the remarkable narrowness of vision in the opposition to a bespoke London bus. I told my two bosses that I was sure I could procure a design to prove the nay-sayers wrong. I was given four pages in the Christmas issue and told to get on with it. I knew where to go for a new bus proposal: Alan Ponsford, boss of the bus and truck designer Capoco. Ponsford very quickly accepted my emailed challenge and – with just a single face-to-face meeting at the Institute of Mechanical Engineers – his team produced the beautiful cutaway design that was shown to Johnson and featured in *Autocar,* as well as *The Times*, on the BBC and elsewhere. Showing Johnson the cutaway engineering illustrations, my only political advice was to not let anyone tell him it couldn't be done, because it could.'

Called the RMXL, Ponsford's design concept was a low-floor bus with a lightweight aluminium space frame that incorporated disabled access through a closing front door behind the front wheels. There was, too, an open-platform rear access, leading directly on to the staircase at the back. *Autocar* had paid Capoco a modest £750 for the design.

Johnson liked the idea in principle and he suggested that he would hold a formal design competition to develop a new Routemaster if he won the May 2008 election. It formed a significant part of his manifesto which also focused on scrapping the bendy buses introduced while Ken Livingstone was mayor; these

The cutaway engineering drawing of Alan Ponsford's 9.8 metre RMXL as it appeared in the Christmas 2007 issue of *Autocar* magazine.

had also suffered severe teething problems, notably a series of fires. These had been remedied and the buses were running efficiently along the main arterial corridors, but some Londoners felt the bendy buses were inappropriate for the narrow streets in central London. They were also regarded as a free service for fare dodgers who did not have to walk past the driver to get on the bus and therefore could avoid using the Oyster reader. Consequently, the political message conveyed by Johnson was that these 'alien' bendy buses would be got rid of to be replaced by an 'iconic' – a word that later became overused in the debate – new Routemaster.

In July 2008, Johnson announced the competition for the new bus with the aim of involving both the industry and the public at large. He called for the new bus design to be 'stylish, spacious and energy efficient' and with an open platform at the back staffed by a second crew member. As part of paying prize money to the winners and runners up, Transport for London purchased the copyright in the designs, permitting the royalty-free use of elements from them in the final design. There were three categories: Whole Design, Design Element and 'Imagine', the last named allowing creative minds to run free without constraints of practicality. The Imagine section was divided into four age groups: Below 11, 11-15, 16-18 and adult. A number of children sent in entries.

The judging panel, overseen by the Mayor, was made up of the Mayor's transport adviser Kulveer Ranger, Transport Commissioner Peter Hendy, TfL's MD of Surface Transport David Brown, London Buses' managers Mike Weston and Clare Kavanagh and bus design consultant David Quainton, formerly marketing director of Alexander Dennis. Quainton's job (unpaid; expenses only) was to sort through the 700-odd entries to decide which ones were worth showing to the rest of the judges. He scored each of the Design entries according to such things as style, innovation, good use of interior space and practicality and making sure they met the specifications that had been laid down. For the Imagine category, the specifications did not apply. The Imagine category called for the submission of imaginative ideas without too much regard for practicality. The Design category was more specific and asked for detailed designs of a low floor red double-decker bus with at least one internal staircase, a rear open platform, and one other entrance with doors, to be crewed by a driver and conductor, and suitable for carrying at least 72 passengers seated and standing. A maximum length of 13.5m was specified and the bus could have up to three axles. It had to be practical and economic and capable of being put into mass production. The competition offered cash prizes for entrants, with £25,000 for the winner, and smaller awards for good ideas in the Imagine category – a total of £80,000.

There were still doubts about whether this was a serious attempt to create a new bus for the capital or whether it was just a sophisticated PR exercise. However, the response, with 225 entries for the Design category and a further 475 in the Imagine category, by the closing date of 19th September 2008 was very enthusiastic. Many of the designs that had been submitted to the competition were of a very high standard and incorporated a number of innovative features.

The results were announced just before Christmas 2008 with the £25,000 prize for the key Design category being shared between Capoco and a joint submission made by architects Foster and Partners and the car manufacturer Aston Martin. The Aston Martin-Foster bus design envisaged a highly-manoeuvrable, zero-emissions 71-seater vehicle, with solar panels built into a polycarbonate-glazed roof, full accessibility, warm lighting and wooden floors. According to Foster, the design was finalised 'after an intense period of research which included canvassing opinion from passengers, drivers and conductors' with the aim of designing 'a new bus from the inside-out'. The Capoco design combined a low flat floor to allow easy access but retaining the Routemaster-style front engine and open rear platform. It had room for 80 passengers, 66 of which were seated.

Alan Ponsford in his Capoco Design studio with his entry contrasted with a Routemaster. His design sought to repeat the lightweight approach of the original with a target unladen weight of 8,200kg (the RML weighed 7874kg and gave an MPG figure of 8–9 in service conditions).

Foster + Partners in association with Aston Martin won first prize jointly with Capoco, whose design is seen opposite. The team of Foster and Aston Martin came up with the kind of style Boris Johnson was looking for and, though totally new to bus design, did a lot of homework to produce an attractive proposal with a number of practical features. Their press release from the time is shown here. The bus would have been powered by a hydrogen fuel cell that would charge batteries distributed within the lower floor construction. It would have zero emissions and be almost silent in operation. It was also designed to be easily upgradable to alternative power units as technology developed. By using electric wheel hub motors, the axle-free design envisaged a low floor throughout the length of the lower deck. How practical all this may have been is open to question. The majority of the lower saloon seats were longitudinal, including two tip-up seats in the wheelchair area. Upstairs at the rear a quarter-circle seat for three people was placed next to the stairs and would follow the curve of the bus. The roof would incorporate lightweight polycarbonate glazing panels running the length of the upper deck and these would have photo-voltaic panels to help charge the batteries. Solar film on the glazing would help control heat gain. The bus design, with lightweight composite material for its bodywork and sustainable materials like leather and wood for the interior, was 10.7m long and seated 71 people.

Foster + Partners with Aston Martin win joint first prize in competition to design a new bus for London

19.12.2008

The joint submission by Foster + Partners and Aston Martin has won first prize, alongside Capoco Design, in Transport for Londons competition to design a new bus for the capital. The two iconic British brands worked together to challenge preconceptions of bus design with a vehicle that is environmentally sensitive, accessible, convivial and reinvents a much-loved symbol of London for the modern era.

After an intense period of research which included canvassing opinion from passengers, drivers and conductors, the two parties worked in close collaboration to design a new bus from the inside-out. In doing so, consideration was given to a wide range of issues including layout, use of materials, motive power, passenger experience and the bus impact on the streetscape and the environment of the city. The bus is designed to navigate the dense and varied streets of London, employing innovative technologies to allow for greater manoeuvrability and energy conservation. Optimising safety, the driver's cabin provides panoramic views as well as incorporating screens to supervise CCTV images and radio communications with the on-board conductor.

Much like a car or a building, the design evolved in response to the needs of its users. The layout, lighting and wooden floors are conceived to encourage a spirit of warmth and community. The arrangement of the decks is driven by comfort and particular consideration is given to the selection of reconstituted leather upholstery to create a tactile living room feel, especially in the saloon-like lower deck.

The new bus is zero emissions ready, accessible for all and will set new standards for sustainable public service vehicles. Passengers benefit from views from the top of the deck through a glazed roof which incorporates solar cells to generate energy and filter daylight to control the temperature inside.

The bus design re-introduces the rear open access platform that made London's Routemaster bus so popular up until its withdrawal from general service. This is supplemented by a side door to facilitate access for the mobility impaired and families with young children.

Lord Foster said:
I am delighted that we have won joint first prize with the Aston Martin/Foster + Partners design. This project has really captured my imagination. Londons buses are so much a part of the essence of this city functionally, symbolically and geographically. They help us draw a mental map their destinations are Londons historic places, often green: Shepherds Bush, Islington Green, Hampstead Heath, Green Park. Our design seeks to combine contemporary innovation with timelessness. Like the original Routemaster which was ahead of its time and consequently endured a new bus for London should establish a whole new travel experience that espouses 21st century aspirations, while celebrating the memory and the experience of the original.

The Hector Serrano Studio, in association with Minarro Garcia and Javier Esteban, was joint second prizewinner and its entry was a firm favourite of Boris Johnson's, according to one correspondent who was at the awards ceremony. It had plug doors at the front for wheelchair users and made reference to the Routemaster in its bonnet and front grille design. The designers aimed to retain the friendly and warm feeling of the RM and it was one of the shortest of the designs submitted, which when coupled with hybrid diesel-electric drive would be low on emissions. The Union Flag patterned wheels were a nice touch. The three design studios from different fields, such as vehicle and product design and visual communication, joined forces. They have received prestigious awards such as the Peugeot Design Awards and their projects have been exhibited extensively in Museums such as the V&A in London and Cooper-Hewit National Design Museum in New York. They set up their offices in London, Barcelona and Valencia after studying at the Royal College of Art in London. More illustrations of this design can be viewed on their website www.hectorserrano.com

Jamie Martin, seen at the awards ceremony, won the other second prize for his solo effort on a modern version of the Routemaster, which he called the London Navigator. It was an early favourite of the judges, who referred to it as a 'bold and modern take on original Routemaster lines'. In the background is project manager David Hampson-Ghani. The bus was designed as a hybrid with rear-axle hub motors. In common with the other second-prize winner, a front entrance for wheelchair users employed plug doors as used on London tube trains. A bio-diesel engine and a radiator were placed between the front wheels and three lithium iron batteries were provided towards the rear, one mounted under the stairs along with the fuel tank.

Peter Hendy, who commissioned bendy buses and was one of their staunchest defenders, said the competition could produce a ground-breaking successor. 'This is a fantastic opportunity for people in the motor vehicle industry to give us buses that are light, durable 21st century vehicles.' One of the competition's entrants, Toby Tinsley, speaks of the task the designers were faced with: 'The function of the bus has to come first. It's not so much about what you can do, it's establishing what you can't do and then trying to make it work. Designing a bus is very different from other vehicles – you can't simply sculpt a beautiful shape around a chassis – there are lots of rules; how many people, front and rear access, disabled access, safety, ease of use and so forth.'

The Routemaster heritage was a feature in many of the designs submitted for the competition. Toby Tinsley and Adrian Dewey had some fundamental things they wanted to push forward in their design – the 'nose' of the bus being one of them. 'A car', said Toby, 'is very recognisable from the shape of the front grille and I wanted to keep the look of the iconic old bus in the new bus, so we took the nose as the starting point and worked back from there. By doing this you strengthen the heritage and familiarity through a modern design'. The sharp diagonal 'strike' on the platform and stairs makes a feature from the internal staircase.

23
Westbourne Park Station
Ladbroke Grove Station
Paddington Station
Trafalgar Square
Aldwych West Arm
Ludgate Circus
Bank Station
Liverpool Street Bus Station
Liverpool Street
LK53 EZD

23

WE ARE LONDONERS
Pay As You Go
23

Opposite: Even in the Design category, some of the designs submitted would have presented serious practical issues. London based designers Pope Wainwright approached the design of their bus 'from the inside out' and it would certainly seem from these illustrations that it would have given good views for passengers. Glass was envisaged that would reduce solar gain in the summer months and provide some insulation during the winter months, though how effective this would have been is open to question.

Raj Nahal was another entrant who included a glazed staircase in his design, also another one to incorporate a Routemaster style front grille. Behind the nearside front wheel is a second entrance.

Reiko Ito is a design studio located in Tokyo and Milan. In the area of vehicle design they have worked on cars, some very futuristic looking mobility vehicles and an electrically assisted bicycle. Like many other entrants to the competition, they had not previously designed a bus. Their bus, with a Union Flag pattern in its window layout, had a glazed centre door that projected (along with the window above it) from the main bodywork in a way that made it look articulated and would have given the rest of the bus a restricted width to fit within the legal maximum. The offside handrail may have been a design feature that balanced the platform handrail aesthetically but it does not appear to be of much practical use.

Royal College of Art student Jukka Rautiainen's design was modern, attractive and distinctive. Tube style gates are shown on the rear platform, which would have delayed boarding and largely removed the point of an open rear entrance. With no rear glazing the platform would probably have been rather gloomy.

Blake Cotterill submitted drawings that were loosely based on a Routemaster design with which he had come second in a World Automotive Design competition a few years earlier. It was heavily adapted to suit the TfL brief. It was one of the submissions to include a small diesel engine to drive an electric generator; the same principle as adopted by Wrightbus.

A sporty look was submitted by Hong Yeo, a design student at the Royal College of Art. A striking appearance sacrificed headroom at the rear of the upper deck.

Opposite: Korean designer Ji Hun Lee submitted an attractive design that paid homage to the Routemaster's predecessor. At the time, he was 28 years of age and studying for his MA in Automotive Design at Coventry University. He developed an interest in buses by visiting Coventry Transport Museum and by riding on classic buses including London RTs. The design was for a bus powered by an electric motor and biodiesel engine.

Finchley Road
Oxford Street
Picadilly Circus
13
GOLDERS GREEN STATION
RT08 LEE

Attractive and gracefully curved as the design from Ji Hun Lee was, a hark back to the RT was not what the judges were looking for and it was eliminated at an early stage.

How to design the perfect bus

What should Boris Johnson be looking out for with a new London bus?

A Routemaster mark 2 shouldn't be a retro version of the bus we loved that was in service in London for half a century.

It needs to be thought out from first principles, and be the most environmentally-friendly bus possible.

But it is not a question of a mere styling exercise.

What mayor Johnson should be looking for is a truly radical bus, just as the Routemaster was the most advanced city bus of its generation in the world. So a Routemaster mark 2 might not look like anything else on the road, and it would be best if it was a bus that could be designed so that it could take on many configurations.

Some new Routemasters might have a conductor and an open platform, others might not, and of course it would be a bus that would have to cope with every level of physical disability.

Unlike the latest wave of double deckers and bendy buses, it also needs to adorn the streets of the city it serves: it should be regarded as a work of mobile architecture, as much as a work of engineering and public service

Jonathan Glancey

Left: Architectural correspondent Jonathan Glancey's views – very similar indeed to TfL's – on what should be looked for in the new bus, published in the Guardian on-line version in the month the competition was announced.

13
Finchley Road
Oxford Street
Picadilly Circus
GOLDERS GREEN STATION
13
RT08 LEE

This very smooth, attractive and radical update of the basic Routemaster shape was submitted by Chris Ashby. It was another to use glazing in areas not normally glazed on buses, reflecting attention being given to the passenger experience as well as the external look. The bonnet was designed to act as a cycle rack for five bikes and the hinged lamps on the nearside front wheel were for the benefit of cyclists when the bus was turning. The bonnet was designed to act as a cycle rack for five bikes and the hinged lamps on the nearside front wheel were for the benefit of cyclists when the bus was turning. A large route display at the rear doubled up as a warning for when the bus was pulling out.

From Germany came this Routemaster update with a chrome radiator grille owing something to the styling of some Rolls-Royce cars. Quite a few of the designs submitted, including this one, would have given poor nearside visibility for the driver.

Associate Editor of *Autocar* magazine Hilton Holloway worked with Rolf Schepp of Lineale Design on this entry for the NBfL competition. The thinking behind the design was to get quite close to the Routemaster, but to give it a much more modernist edge in the same way Land Rover re-invented the Discovery with the Mk3 model. The nose design refers to the classic grille design of the RM, but treats it in a much more minimalist style, pushing it back instead of standing proud. The wrap-around cockpit is also a reference to the RM's half cab. The sloping and heavily glazed front end of the upper deck was partly designed to give the bus a more modern and dynamic feel. A scrolling LED sign in the central band would have shown the bus's route.

Tata Elxsi Ltd has its main base in India and is a major supplier of buses to Asian customers. For maximum capacity and boarding and alighting speeds, together with the provision of a cycle rack (visible behind the centre doors), they produced a three-axle design with three doors. Though including a bow to the Routemaster in its bonnet and radiator grille design, it lacks the grace of some of the other entries.

Concrete All Round Design also submitted a three axle-design, this one employing smaller wheels at the rear, both of which were steered to overcome wheel scrub. The design enabled a flat floor throughout. Power would be by a combination of hydrogen cells mounted in the ceiling of the bus and high power batteries.

Ogle Noor is a UK based design company which had a previous connection with London buses, Ogle Designs being appointed by London Transport in the mid-1980s when they were commissioned to undertake research and design work on bus interior layouts. For the 2008 competition they submitted this attractive and curvaceous design with a large roundel each side that illuminated, along with advertising, at night. The centre doors are barely visible in these views, but were cut into the left side of the roundel.

Winners

Category	Type	Prize	Prize value		Ref	Name	Organisation	Location	No in party
Design	**Whole**	1st =	£	25,000	708616	Alan Ponsford	Capoco Design Ltd	Salisbury	5
		1st =	£	25,000	727673	Todd Hutton	Foster & Partners/Aston Martin Ltd	London	5
		2nd =	£	10,000	727689	Hector Serrano	Hector Serrano Studio	London	4
		2nd =	£	10,000	724455/1	Jamie Martin	N/A	Surbiton	4
		merit 1	£	2,000	724383/1	David Bradshaw	N/A	Nottingham	3
		merit 2	£	2,000	724528	Martyn Collar	Style to Design Ltd	Coventry	3
		merit 3	£	2,000	726614/1	Alexander Crolla & Pieter Lasage	Concrete All Round Creative	Antwerp, Belgium	3
		merit 4	£	2,000	724578	Andrew Plumb	LA:UK Design Ltd	Crewe	3
		merit 5	£	2,000	727841	Eric Woodcock	N/A	Southport	3
		Totals	£	80,000					33
	Element	Merit 1	£	500	601326/2	Lotti Duke		Lancaster	4
		Merit 2	£	500	724669	Rhys Whyman		Cheshunt	4
		Totals	£	1,000					8
Imagine	**< 11**	1st =	£	200	725807	Thomas Staricoff		Brighton	4
		1st =	£	200	724667	Olivier Carrier		London	4
		2nd	£	90	713985	Luke Brennan		East Barnet	4
		3rd	£	65	726611	Yasmin Ali		Plaistow	4
		Merit 1	£	50	725720	Hanna Broadhurst		Bromley	4
		Merit 2	£	50	725720	Takeo Broadhurst		Bromley	
	11 - 15	1st	£	300	725785	Dolapo Okunlola		Peckham	4
		2nd	£	90	724442	Ben Holmes		St Albans	4
		3rd	£	65	714071/1	Albert Braid		Crystal Palace	4
	16 - 18	1st	£	500	723824	Nicholas Cho		Crowthorne	4
		2nd	£	90	724340/1	Craig Tomkins		Eastleigh	4
		3rd	£	65	718260	Charlotte Taylor		Fetcham	4
	> 18	1st	£	1,000	727884	Frances Faulder		Kilburn	4
		2nd	£	500	723361/1	Matt Becher		Warwick	4
		3rd	£	250	725784	Alan Thorley		Billericay	4
		Merit 1	£	100	725956/1	Vas Laszlo		London	2
		Totals	£	3,615					58
		Grand total	£	84,615					99

List of prizewinners in the public competition.

There had been a general belief among the designers that the winner of the competition would see his or her design progressed to produce the finished bus – indeed many of the entrants would not have devoted so much time to it had they thought otherwise. It became clear at the time the prizewinners were announced that no single idea would be used but that all the ideas would be looked at for feeding into the final design, which would be subject to a separate tender process. In Transport Commissioner Peter Hendy's words: 'What we should aim to create now is not just a Routemaster replacement but a whole new generation of London buses that could affect the future of the entire industry'. He went on to say that the process could not be rushed and that the end result might be more radical than anyone had yet proposed.

While the designs – particularly the one involving prestige car maker Aston Martin – attracted considerable interest in the press, there were still some strong dissenting voices. Val Shawcross, the Labour member for transport on the Greater London Assembly, dismissed the whole idea: 'The design competition may have been fun and the winning designs are extremely impressive, but this is not a serious way to make policy and not a worthwhile use of public money. I have yet to hear one convincing argument for why London needs a new double-decker bus and until Boris comes up with some, Londoners will see this as little more than a vanity project.'

There was understandable nervousness about the requirement to have an open platform. This was 2008, not fifty years earlier. In a compensation culture, would TfL be responsible if someone, perhaps under the influence of drink, did not quite manage to hop on the bus and found themselves under the wheels of the vehicle instead? Such nervousness overlooked the fact that deaths of passengers have occurred by their getting trapped in the centre doors of buses.

The concerns were dismissed and Johnson and TfL pressed ahead with developing a bus. The winning entries were passed by TfL to bus manufacturers for them to draw up detailed final designs meeting all relevant legislation, and later presented to TfL for consideration on a competitive-tender basis. In April 2009, a formal invitation to express interest in the project was published in the *Official Journal of the European Union* which is a legal requirement for any tenders above around £200,000. Six bus manufacturers were the following month invited to negotiate for the contract to design and build the new bus: Alexander Dennis, EvoBus (which included Mercedes-Benz buses), Hispano Carrocera, Optare, Scania AB and Wrightbus. In contrast to the competition specifications, the contract called for a bus with a capacity for at least 87 passengers, two staircases, three doors, and an open rear platform able to be closed off when not required, such as at night. The bus would be a hybrid, about 11 metres long, utilising technology to make it 40 per cent more fuel efficient than conventional diesel buses, and 15 per cent more fuel efficient than London hybrid buses already in operation. The winner would have to have the capability of building 600 buses over three years.

Two of the six dropped out quickly: Scania reckoned the timetable for the introduction of the prototype was not feasible, while EvoBus had concerns over its lack of double-decker experience. Then Hispano Carrocera dropped out and, eventually, after Optare announced in November 2009 that it was 'no longer in the running', the list was whittled down to just two: Alexander Dennis and Wrightbus.

The final submissions were received by TfL from the two remaining in the contest on 4th December 2009. Alexander Dennis went to the length of submitting three different three-door body designs: one from the Aston Martin and Foster partnership, one from Capoco Design and one of their own (see pages 23-25) while Wrights submitted just an in-house design. Wrightbus had been seen as an outsider because it was principally a bus body builder, rather than whole bus manufacturer, using chassis from established companies such as Volvo and Scania. A clue may have been provided in a visit by Peter Hendy to Wright's Northern Ireland factory to inspect their forthcoming Gemini 2 hybrid at the beginning of October. He did not take the trouble to visit ADL. The contract for the bus was awarded to Wrightbus on 23rd December 2009.

There was even more surprise the following month when TfL announced that it was Heatherwick Studio (which had not been involved in the original bid) that had been appointed to help Wrightbus produce the final design. The result of the process, therefore, was that the two designs which had won the competition were edged out in the final choice by a bus body building company which required a designer, not involved in the competition or the bidding process, to help produce the bus.

WRIGHTBUS v ALEXANDER DENNIS

STEWART J BROWN

As mentioned in the previous chapter, by the end of 2009 the potential manufacturers of the new bus had been reduced to two, Alexander Dennis (ADL) and Wrightbus, who between them were already supplying the bulk of the buses used on London routes. They were for a number of reasons the obvious choices, including the scale of their operations and that, as established suppliers of buses to London, they knew not just the decision-makers at TfL, but also the operators who would be running the buses.

A contract for 600 buses of an advanced design for one of the world's great capital cities carries considerable prestige. But when you spread that over three years it equals just four buses a week – four buses to a unique specification unlikely to interest other cities. One of the potential bidders, EvoBus, is part of the Daimler organisation which builds almost 40,000 buses a year. Scania's annual bus production is approaching 9,000 vehicles. No company likes to turn away potentially profitable business, but for global manufacturers the attraction of building one bus a day for one customer must be limited.

The other British builder in the running, Optare, was in 2009 in the throes of reorganisation and it is doubtful if, at that time, it had the resources to handle such a challenging contract. While both ADL and Wrightbus are significant exporters, they are not global automotive giants. So a 600-vehicle order is significantly more important to their businesses than it would have been to some of those who had been in the running.

Optare dropped out of the manufacturers' competition at a late stage, leaving just ADL and Wrightbus in the running. However, between 2000 and 2005 Optare had been developing a side-engined double-decker design with provision for three doors, clearly aimed at the London market. Fran Cush, who went on to work with Alan Ponsford on the Capoco 2008 competition entry, designed a distinctive and attractive body that puts the company's latest MetroDecker (see page 173) rather in the shade. The designer tells us that weight issues were the main reason the design did not progress.

An Alexander Dennis Enviro 400 and a Wrightbus Gemini at Charing Cross. These designs were the most common London types at the time of the competition for the New Bus for London and this remained the case when the LTs began to enter service. Both evolved from earlier designs from both companies; a complete break from what had gone before was called for in the mayor's new bus. The new design did, however, need to be future-proof in not only suiting Boris Johnson but also future mayors.

ADL had aligned itself with the two first prizewinners in the open competition, Fosters and Capoco, to produce two of its proposals for a complete bus, which would have been based around the company's Enviro400H hybrid double-decker. This used proven components which could have helped cut costs and expedite production. It came as a surprise therefore when Northern Ireland based Wrightbus, with limited experience in chassis manufacture and with few hybrid sales, was selected as the builder of the New Bus for London, as it was then called. ADL's pragmatic approach, developing the new design around existing units, was beaten by the willingness of Wrightbus to start with a clean sheet of paper.

Both manufacturers had been supplying buses to London for some 25 years. ADL predecessor Dennis had established itself as a major force in London first with the Dart midibus, supplying large numbers in the 1990s, and then from 1999 with the double-deck Trident. Bodybuilder Alexander won a number of orders in the 1990s, and became a major supplier from the end of the decade with its ALX400 double-deck body for low-floor chassis.

Wright – as the company was then known – started supplying London at the end of the 1980s, with bodies on Renault S75 and Dennis Dart chassis. Where other bodybuilders used conventional aluminium framing for their bodies, Wright chose a system developed by Alusuisse in which a deep aluminium extrusion ran the full length of the bus below the window line and was a key component in the strength of the structure. Wright further developed this to create its Aluminique system with its R3 split pillar in which the bottom section of the body pillar – the area most vulnerable to damage in minor traffic accidents – can be easily removed and replaced, reducing downtime and repair costs.

But apart from its distinctive construction methods, one of the hallmarks of Wright has been its willingness to innovate. The first low-floor buses in London, 68 Dennises and Scanias in 1994, were bodied by Wright, some of which were for Peter Hendy's CentreWest company. Wright has been the only UK volume producer of articulated buses, on Volvo and Scania chassis. The first serious trial of artics in London, by First CentreWest in 2001, involved Wright-bodied Volvos. The company was also a pioneer in the exploration of alternative power sources, producing a hybrid single-decker, the Electrocity, with a Capstone microturbine as its power source as long ago as 2001. And it was selected by First to build the impressive articulated StreetCar. According to Hendy's foreword in *The Wright Way*, the story of the company, Wright's had been dismantling an old Routemaster 'to learn the lessons of the past in a bid to be part of the future' while the public competition was going on in 2008.

Yet being a pioneer did not always pay off. When low-floor single-deckers became the London standard, very few were bodied by Wright as operators chose the Dennis Dart SLF, typically with Plaxton bodywork. When articulated buses came to the capital they were built in Germany, not in Northern Ireland. And, as history shows, the microturbine was not the way forward for hybrid drive systems. The Electrocity name was revived in 2006 for a batch of hybrids delivered to Go-Ahead London. These were not a success as their small diesel engines were unable to cope with the demands of intensive bus operation. They were later fitted with Cummins engines while retaining a hybrid drive, and this solved the problem. Wrightbus has also supplied the only hydrogen-fuelled buses currently running in Britain, operated in London by Tower Transit and based on chassis supplied by VDL.

While Wright has been steadily growing over the last two decades, the early 2000s were a difficult period for Alexander and Dennis, which in 2001 were united in common ownership by the Mayflower group and renamed TransBus International. Mayflower collapsed in 2004, and the main part of what had been TransBus International emerged as ADL. TransBus did develop one model aimed at London, the original Enviro200. This – foreshadowing the NBfL – had its Cummins engine in the rear offside corner which made room for an exit door in the rear overhang. One of its most unusual features was the use of larger wheels at the rear than at the front. This permitted the use of Super single tyres at the rear, making room for a wide step-free gangway running the full length of the bus. This version of the Enviro200 got no further than two prototypes. It was a victim of the Mayflower collapse, but was also the wrong bus for the time. London was moving away from single-deckers to double-deckers, and no operator outside the capital wanted a bus with an exit in the rear overhang.

Hybrid buses first appeared in London in 2005 when Go Ahead London took a small batch of pioneering Wrightbus Electrocity single deckers. Travel London followed with a handful in 2007, one of which is shown here. The original engines proved unreliable, but the buses ran well with Go Ahead when re-engined and a further six were taken into stock in 2011 for route 360.

While ADL and its Alexander predecessor has been building double-deckers for 70 years, Wrightbus only started building double-deckers in 2001, its first order being 50 on Volvo B7L chassis for Arriva London. The company has continued to work closely with Volvo in the production of double-deckers, including Volvo's B5LH hybrid. But it started offering its own complete double-decker in 2008, using chassis supplied by VDL. The first hybrid versions, the Gemini 2 HEV, entered service with First in London at the end of that year. For the New Routemaster Wrightbus is building its own chassis, and in the summer of 2013 commissioned a purpose-built factory to do this. As well as building the New Routemaster, this factory has the capacity to handle other products.

The ADL business which emerged from the failure of Mayflower was revitalised and immediately set about producing a range of new models, including a double-decker with a Dennis-built chassis and an Alexander-built body, the Enviro400. Close co-operation between chassis and body designers helped optimise the internal layout and to maximise the number of seats in the lower saloon. The Enviro400 quickly proved a success in London and elsewhere, both with conventional diesel and hybrid drive trains, the latter being the Enviro400H. And while ADL lost out on the NBfL contract, it continues to be a major supplier of double-deckers to the capital with the Enviro models. Today ADL is the UK's biggest bus and coach manufacturer, with 2,300 employees. Wrightbus employs 1,400 people.

ADL is the leading supplier of hybrid buses in the UK, with almost 700 in service. While Wrightbus was the first to deliver hybrids to London, with its Electrocity single-deckers in 2006, ADL was the first with hybrid double-deckers, delivering Enviro400Hs to Go-Ahead and Metroline in 2008. The first Wrightbus hybrids, for Arriva, followed in 2009. London has Europe's biggest fleet of hybrid buses, followed by Manchester and Barcelona.

Outside London, ADL has scored considerable success with Stagecoach, which runs almost 240 Enviro400Hs and a small number of Enviro350H single-deckers. ADL has also supplied Enviro400Hs to, among others, First Glasgow, Lothian Buses, East Yorkshire, Reading Buses, National Express in the West Midlands and Dundee, and Go-Ahead subsidiary Oxford Bus Company. There are no complete Wrightbus hybrids in operation outside London other than StreetCars in Las Vegas.

To set their businesses in a global context, both ADL and Wrightbus have been expanding outside the UK. ADL acquired Australian bus bodybuilder Custom Coaches in 2012 but it closed in 2014. The company also has links with Kiwi Bus in New Zealand and with North American manufacturer New Flyer, both of which sell buses based on the Enviro200. In 2013, Wrightbus set up new links with manufacturers in India and Europe. In Europe VDL is to sell the Wrightbus StreetLite midibus, while in India Wrightbus is working in association with Daimler to build buses for the local market.

The New Routemaster is undeniably an important vehicle. It has created a tremendous amount of interest. It has boosted employment at Wrightbus. But it is, and looks set to remain, a niche market product. As with the original Routemaster which inspired it, there look set to be few buyers for it outside the city for which it was built.

For the manufacturers' competition that followed the public design competition, Alexander Dennis Ltd submitted three sets of proposals; one it had commissioned from Foster + Partners and Aston Martin, illustrated on this page, one from Capoco Design and one set of in-house designs. The Foster design had echoes of its earlier competition entry but had three sets of doors. The front doors were of fold-in type, the centre doors were plug type and the rear platform had a combination of fold-in and slide-in doors. Like the other ADL submissions, the bus would have been built on a version of the tried and tested Enviro400H chassis.

Inside the Foster + Partners and Aston Martin design the seating broke away from contemporary trends in bus interior seat frames to echo the Routemaster's. Indeed, the seats, with chrome handrails, can be viewed as individual versions of the RM's bench seats, albeit with less substantial upholstery. The grooved flooring is reminiscent of the Treadmaster flooring used in RMs. At the back a large rear upper deck window shed daylight on the staircase, and on the platform a rear window with a sloping lower frame gave way to a tinted window to give a level of privacy to passengers climbing and descending the stairs.

Capoco Design created this attractive body for ADL, which it called the London Liner, looking more like a luxury double deck coach than a bus.

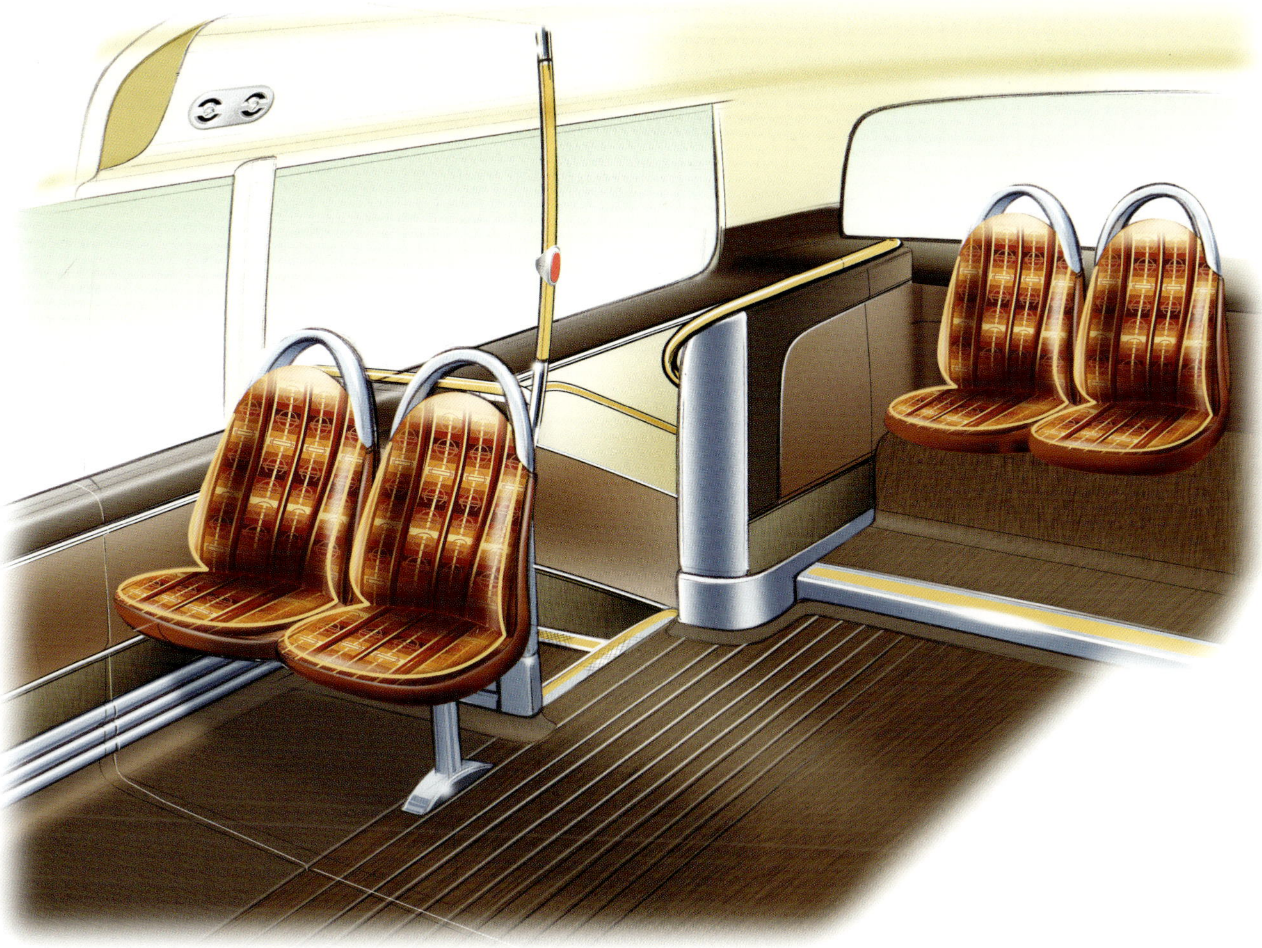

These three drawings from Capoco's final submission for the visual appearance show an attractive interior with window framing towards the rear having some similarity to the treatment on the RT. It has an unmistakably modern look though. The seating moquette cleverly incorporates the TfL roundel. The interior is softened by the skilful use of curves and handrails in two colours.

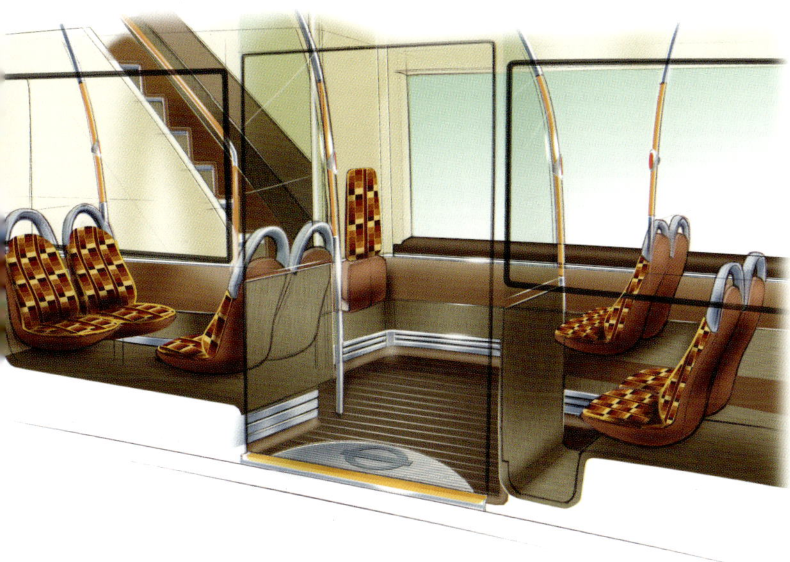

In the new specifications laid down for the design, the bus was to have a minimum capacity of 87 made up of 22 seats in the lower saloon, 40 in the upper and a minimum of 25 standees. Two staircases and three doors were specified, with the rear platform being able to be operated in open mode. Special attention was to be given to making the interior as quiet as possible and free of rattles. The design of a new and unique seating moquette would also be required when the contract was awarded. A prototype bus was to be delivered and placed into trial running by spring 2011 with five delivered and ready for service by January 2012 (later amended to the end of April 2012). The in-house design by ADL came in four alternative varieties with minor differences. An attractive vehicle, 11.1 metres long, it and the other ADL offers lost out to TfL's drive for mechanical innovation.

The interior of ADL's in-house design, received by TfL on 4th December 2009, employed LED lighting and similar window framing to the New Routemaster, but with deeper windows. Overall, a restful appearance was achieved for the inside of the bus, but with little imagination applied to the seating.

For its submission, Wrights included a variety of frontal treatments. Three are shown here to illustrate the alternative ideas they proposed for the windscreen.

In May 2008, within days of Boris Johnson's election victory, Wright's had decided, with encouragement from TfL, to acquire an old RM to dismantle in order to learn from its structural techniques. It was the start of a process that was to lead to the company being given the contract to manufacture the New Bus for London. For the 2009 manufacturer's competition they produced a competent in-house design, with minor alternative variations, but not one that would stand out from other buses on the streets. Under the skin though was a solidly designed body structure of which Wrightbus was so confident they were able to give a 12-year structural warranty. The stylish, chunky window pillars inside the NBfL and bonded glazing were a Wright's feature, though Heatherwick did not take much from the external appearance when they were brought in. The headlamp arrangement survived and the asymmetrical windscreen was further developed.

HEATHERWICK

JAMES WHITING

If Peter Hendy was a major influence in the choice of Wrightbus to build the NBfL, then the deputy chairman of TfL Daniel Moylan was a major player in the appointment of Heatherwick Studio to design the bodywork. Moylan became chairman of the mayor's Design Advisory Panel (mostly concerned with the built environment) in December 2009 and was well aware of the quality of Heatherwick's work, having spoken highly of it whilst a councillor with the Royal Borough of Kensington and Chelsea.

In January 2010, very soon after the contract had been signed with Wrightbus for building the new bus, Heatherwick Studio was selected by TfL to handle the design of the bodywork and interior detailing. The Kings Cross based studio had been formed in 1994 by Thomas Heatherwick and over the past 20 years has achieved a reputation for cutting edge design. Heatherwick, 39 at the time he was appointed, graduated from the Royal College of Art where he studied furniture design. His capacity for original thinking had become apparent while he was a student at Manchester Polytechnic, where he built a full-size and futuristic looking pavilion in the grounds.

Heatherwick chose as his project leader on the new bus Stuart Wood, who had joined the studio in 2001. Stuart's particular expertise is with 3D computer-aided design work and he also has extensive knowledge of manufacturing processes. He was assisted throughout the design process by the studio's Neil Hubbard. A visit to the Wrightbus factory in Northern Ireland to see buses being built was an important part of the exercise. In Neil's words: 'The great thing about the factory is that you kind of have a mock-up at every stage – you see the production line from chassis level, as they fit the components, up to finished bus'.

It was Wrightbus's job to satisfy the engineering and practical aspects, and Heatherwick's job to satisfy the mayor with an 'iconic' appearance for the new bus. Thomas Heatherwick was a good choice for the job, despite (or perhaps because of) his own admission that he 'knew nothing about buses'. This guaranteed fresh thinking and the bus that has resulted certainly stands out as unlike any other bus on London's streets – or streets elsewhere for that matter.

The benefit to Stuart and Neil of the factory visit was shared by Wrightbus. According to David Barnett, the company's Development Engineering Manager, they learnt from the team the approach of starting with a blank sheet of paper and asking 'why' for each different component on the bus. For some of these there was nothing set in legislation; they had just evolved into the company's standard way of doing things whenever they were designing a bus.

The total fees for the design were £427,500, made up of £50,000 for the design principles, £85,000 for the external design, £150,000 for the interior styling and the balance of £142,500 for the studio's prototyping costs, design support during build and monitoring of the bus up to the delivery of the certified prototype.

One of a series of TfL computer generated images of the design released to the media in May 2010. At about the same time, work began at the Wrightbus factory on the full size mock-up. Heatherwick had never been involved in bus design and Wright's had never worked with an outside designer, but the mix worked.

According to Barnett, the brief the team was given was: 'If you walk out of the TfL offices to the nearest postcard stand you will find a few iconic images on a postcard; a black taxi, a red phone box and a Routemaster bus. Fast forward five years and you will see a black cab, a red phone box and your design as the iconic London transport image'.

The starting point for Heatherwick, as specified by TfL, was the front and rear end treatment. Wrights had worked on the basic structure of the body and had produced its own body design also, but its look was not what Boris Johnson was seeking. Heatherwick's job was to transform it into an iconic design. Early sketches show the front and rear glazing extending to floor level on the nearside, generous curves in the front and rear domes and shallow upper-deck windows. Style was paramount. However, the shallow upper-deck windows also aimed to reduce the effect of the sun on the interior temperature. A stylish flow was given to the front of the bus by wrapping round the front upper deck windows and having the driver's windscreen sweep down from offside to nearside. The beautifully sweeping glazed rear, Heatherwick's favourite part of the bus, invites passengers on to the upper deck and echoes the open-staircase buses of the 1920s.

The unveiling to the press of the computer aided drawings of the exterior design was held at Battersea bus garage on 17th May 2010 at which time the interior was still being finalised. Here, people learned that a full size static mock up was being worked on for completion later in the year. Boris Johnson, who performed the unveiling with Peter Hendy, spoke of the new bus as not only beautiful but also having a 'green heart beating beneath its stylish, swooshing exterior'.

The previous month, TfL was still seeking reassurance from the Department for Transport that the bus, in its planned configuration, would get approval to operate. Conditional reassurance came in an email dated 12th April from the DfT to the project's leader David Hampson-Ghani, following a visit to the Department's offices by the bus's technical consultant Chris Dyal. The DfT's Donald Macdonald wrote to say that they had 'reached a conclusion which gives more confidence about the approval of this vehicle design' (doubts had been expressed earlier). He questioned whether TfL was planning to seek approval at European level and continued: 'While we believe that there is no impediment to the approval of an open platform design with two different modes of operation, the European approach would perhaps result in a greater level of scrutiny by other member states and the European Commission, simply because such approvals have validity throughout the EC'. Further contacts between TfL and the DfT took place on the matter but, as things turned out, there was to be no impediment put in the way of the bus either by the UK licensing authority or by Europe. EC Whole Vehicle Type Approval was later granted.

Originally, it had been planned that the forward staircase would be of similar layout to the Wright Gemini and common to London buses generally; that is with just the bottom step angled towards the centre door. At the request of London Travelwatch, one of the organisations that prompted modifications, two steps at the foot of the staircase were turned 90 degrees to the higher ones, giving as a by-product a little more floor space. The main reason for the request was to reduce the potential distance someone could fall on the stairs. At one point, according to a contemporary report, the upper deck layout provided for an area free of seating at the top of these stairs, with a double seat on the nearside only at the front. When the mock up was built, the only seat fitted to the bus in the front three-quarters of the upper deck was the one at the front offside so if it was ever planned to omit this, the plan had been superseded by then.

In Heatherwick's own words, quoted here from the Studio's press release, 'The geometry of the vehicle developed from a series of pragmatic decisions. It was in order to minimise the perceived size of the vehicle that its corners and edges were rounded. It was to allow the driver to see small children standing next to the bus that its front window was angled down towards the pavement. And, with its three doors on one side and two staircases on the other, it was the functional asymmetry of the bus's internal circulation that led to its asymmetrical geometry. The windows form two ribbons of glass that wrap around the bus, corresponding to the two staircases, which transform the stairs from a dark constricted tunnel to a different kind of space.

'In recent years, bus interiors had grown increasingly chaotic, with their peculiar seating arrangements, fluorescent yellow handrails, over-bright strip lighting and protruding lumps of machinery encased in mysterious fibre-glass housings. The aim was to recalibrate the countless compromises that had accumulated over the years to create an interior that felt as calm as co-ordinated as possible. Using a simple palette of colours and materials, a family of details was developed that included new stairs, lighting, hand poles and stop buttons. We argued for a return to bench type seats that two people could share and designed a new pattern of moquette'.

The full size mock up of the NBfL was built at the Ballymena factory and shipped across the Irish Sea, as the buses themselves would be starting a year later. It was constructed using mostly the materials of a real bus for its body shell and placed on a scrap Scania chassis. It could however be moved by low loader only, not towed. The mock up was given the classification MN0123, MN being the initials of Wright's managing director Mark Nodder. The registration letters were reportedly chosen by project leader Hampson-Ghani as of personal significance. It was transported, unsheeted despite an air of secrecy, to the London Transport Museum's Acton depot at the beginning of November 2010 in readiness for it to be shown to the press, TfL bus staff and service contractors and passenger groups for their comments. At a launch on 11th November, attended by Johnson, Peter Hendy and the Secretary of State for Northern Ireland, Owen Paterson, those present got their first view of the bus in life-size form. Boris, clearly delighted with the end result, described the bus as 'delectable' and 'amazing'.

Parked alongside earlier London bus designs from the Museum's collection, the mock up made an impressive sight. The responses from those who visited it at Acton during its period there were mostly positive and almost everyone spoke well of the exterior appearance. Visitors included members of the London Assembly, senior transport officers of the London boroughs, the bus operating companies and unions, London Travelwatch, and a number of groups representing passengers with special needs – mobility groups on behalf of wheelchair users, those concerned with the welfare of people with learning difficulties, and the Royal National Institutes for the Blind and the Deaf. The interior made extensive use of plywood and a maximum of four people were permitted upstairs.

The mock up, the first one of full size that Wrights had produced, gave those who saw it their first look at the interior of the bus. Off-the-street participants in the survey were given a £5 shopping voucher. There were echoes of the Routemaster in the double bench seating (but with separate sets of cushions for each seated passenger), the colouring of the seat fabric and walls and in the Treadmaster cork-resin flooring used on the front and rear platforms. Back in 1952/3 a full size mock up had also been built for the original RM.

Overleaf The mock up was exhibited alongside earlier London buses from the LT Museum collection.

LONDON TRANSPORT
RCL 2229
RF 537
world
itement.

Liverpool Street 23
BUS STOP
Great Winchester Street
towards
Liverpool Street Station
11
23
N11
BU12 HHJ
T567

LT1676

Opposite and left
Between the display of the mock up and the building of the prototypes, a few other changes were made, including handrails being added to the raised seats in the lower deck, a 'next stop' electronic display added to the nearside rear bulkhead for the benefit of passengers in the rear facing seats and the seat edges finished in a striped moquette pattern rather than plain red. The brackets that can be seen on the window pillars just forward of the raised seating were for the fitting of bracing during the mock up's transit. Four different moquette patterns are used on the NBfL, three of which are variations on the same theme: one for the seat cushions and two for the different heights of seat back. The fourth uses the same colours but is a plain pattern of solid rectangles used for the sides of the seat cushions (though not on the mock up) and the wheelchair area. Up to the time the mock up was built, the 'Buses' roundel had not appeared on buses.

Groups representing wheelchair users had the most comments in terms of possible alterations and there was some pressure for the new bus to have two wheelchair spaces to allow for the fact that wheelchair users sometimes like to travel with friends who are also wheelchair-bound. It was pointed out that not only was it necessary to balance the needs of all users but that a second wheelchair space was not possible because there was insufficient flat floor area available. Only one change was made to the mock up while at Acton; the pole between the wheelchair bay and the centre door was modified in January 2011 to improve accessibility. It was also agreed that an additional horizontal handrail half way up the front staircase would be fitted to the buses when built and that the gold-coloured handrails would be slightly more yellow to assist the visually impaired. The horizontal bar between the wheelchair area and the offside bench seat was removed as an obstruction to mothers with children in pushchairs. The lower deck ceiling of the bus is 2060mm from the floor to allow headroom for the raised seats at the rear; this compares with 1840mm in an Enviro 400.

The upper deck was mostly empty of seating; there was one pair of seats in front of the forward staircase and five pairs at the back. The rest was an empty floor. A major criticism was about the height of the ceiling upstairs. Of a sample of 127 people questioned, 46% said it was a little too low and 19% much too low. The ceiling was indeed lower above the seats (but not in the aisle) and the effect was probably exaggerated to some extent by the fact that there was no natural light entering the mock up and the artificial light that was provided could make it feel quite claustrophobic.

Seat spacing took quite a lot of thought, Heatherwick aiming to give as many passengers as possible a good view through the windows (no two of which on each side are the same width). This aim has been achieved more successfully on the upper deck than downstairs, where the scope for avoiding thick window pillars in the line of view was much more limited, the seat positions being dictated by the door positions, the axles and the wheelchair space. The least satisfactory seat is perhaps the rear-facing offside one on the lower deck where the forward view is of the blank wall between the saloon and the engine compartment. There are no forward facing passenger seats ahead of the centre door and only six altogether downstairs compared to ten facing the back. Again this is unavoidable in view of the chassis layout. Some have commented that more headroom, and less of a step up to the seats, at the rear of the lower deck would have been achieved by having inward facing bench seats (as on the RM and some of the competition entries). However, the width of the wheelarches prevented this, the offside one including the drive to the generator.

Opposite The upper deck of the mock up, devoid of most of the seating and without the distinctive lighting, did not look particularly inviting. Only the rear section was complete in its furnishing. The chrome RM style seat frames gave way to black painted ones on the real buses. Variations of the moquette design were tried out prior to making the final choice.

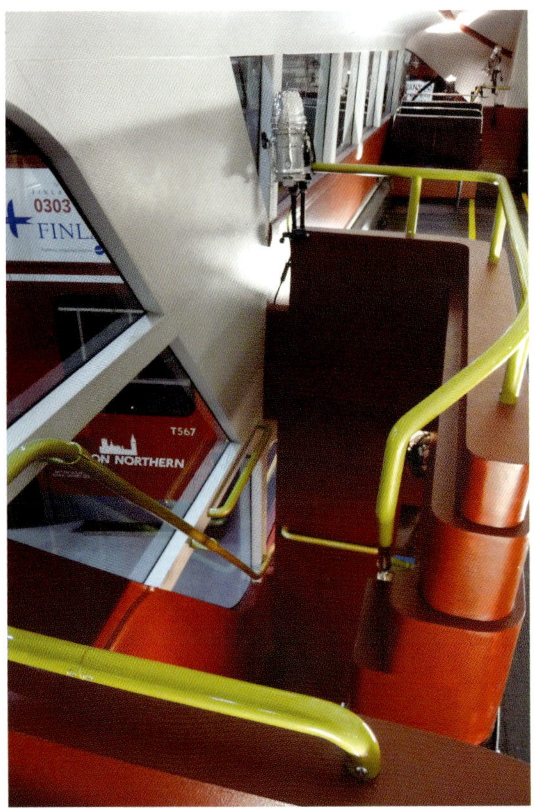

The forward stairs of the mock up. The Oyster card reader at the foot of the stairs was moved when the prototypes were built and the handrail on the right in the second photograph made shallower.

The mock up at Covent Garden, where many more people were able to see it and compare it with older London buses at the Museum. Note the somewhat neater tree guard on the mock up.

After four months at Acton, the mock up was moved to the Museum's main Covent Garden site in March where it could be seen by a wider public. It was on display there until the end of November when it was moved for storage, and possible use of body parts, to London General's Mandela Way East garage.

When the prototypes appeared there was very little difference between them and the mock up, the exact provision and positioning of handrails being one of the minor changes. In the finished buses, though, it was possible to appreciate fully the styling and how it feels to the passenger. The interior colour scheme's more traditional feel, using burgundy and soft white, has been well received. The burgundy was used for the lower half of the walls and as the base colour for the seats, so that the bus would 'look good dirty'. 'If it's a slushy, winter day,' explained Heatherwick, 'and seventy schoolkids get on, the floor is going to get covered in salty slush, and the seats might have a bit of kebab or whatever.' Specific comments from people who had inspected the mock up varied from 'Stylish patterning' and 'Appealing retro look' to 'Colours unappealing' and 'Too old fashioned'. Overall, about three-quarters of those questioned liked the seat fabric colour and design.

Lighting is also a break away from modern trends in bus design. Although the first computer-generated illustrations produced by TfL, those issued to the press in May 2010, included one night-time impression with the interior lit by fluorescent tubes, this form of lighting was never intended. Fluorescent lighting, said Heatherwick, was the least flattering form of light to human tissue: 'It's what you have on a battery chicken farm'. So it was shunned in favour of circular LED lights placed at intervals along the ceilings. These create a more restful environment after dark than bright fluorescent tubes.

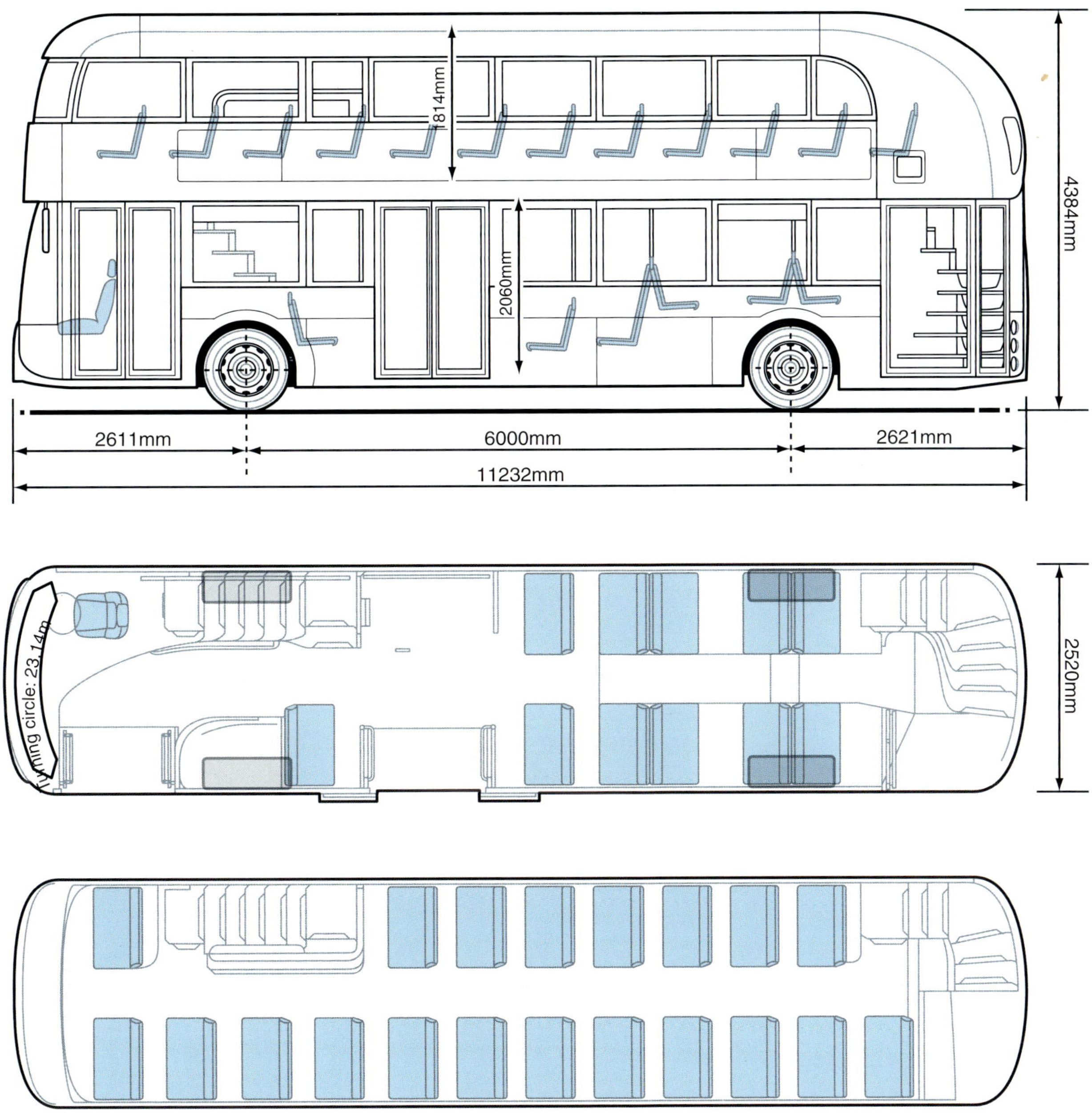

The decision to have non-opening windows that was to cause problems when the bus entered service was not left to Heatherwick; indeed in an interview for the *Daily Telegraph* in June 2011 he lamented: 'Buildings used to have windows that opened, trains used to have windows that opened, but now more and more things are sealed and enclosed'. At the launch of the first prototype at the end of that year, the press were told that no decision had been made on whether the production vehicles would have opening windows, so the performance of the cooling system on the prototypes was intended to inform this decision. However the plain windows certainly contribute to the sleek appearance of the bus, and opening windows upstairs would interfere with the passenger's view in a way that other modern double-deckers with their taller windows do not. The main reason non-openers were decided on however was to avoid interference with the air cooling system.

The finished dimensions of the bus and the seating layouts downstairs and upstairs. These drawings show well why it was necessary to employ a slightly greater than ideal length for the new bus if capacity was not to be compromised. All space available for seating is used and a length more normal on London double deckers of 10.6m would have given eight fewer seats.

The styling upstairs is somewhat different from that downstairs. On the upper deck, in common with the designers of the Virgin Pendolino trains, Heatherwick went for an aircraft feel. The lower deck interior, with many more constraints on the layout and design, is more workmanlike and functional, though the ceiling, window frames and seats follow the same style. The rear end is very distinctive, not least because of the diagonal glazing that extends to the upper deck. Despite the presence of the engine compartment under the stairs there is a shallow set-back area that was also a feature in the Routemaster design as a place for the conductor to stand out of the way of passengers boarding or alighting. In practice this has proved to be a very warm place for the conductor to stand; welcome perhaps in the winter months.

The gold-coloured stanchions, which smoothly incorporate the wireless bell pushes, are a nice touch, as also are the burgundy-coloured Oyster card readers. Heatherwick had originally hoped that faux leather could be used for these, but this material was not considered the most practical, an example of the small compromises that had to be accepted.

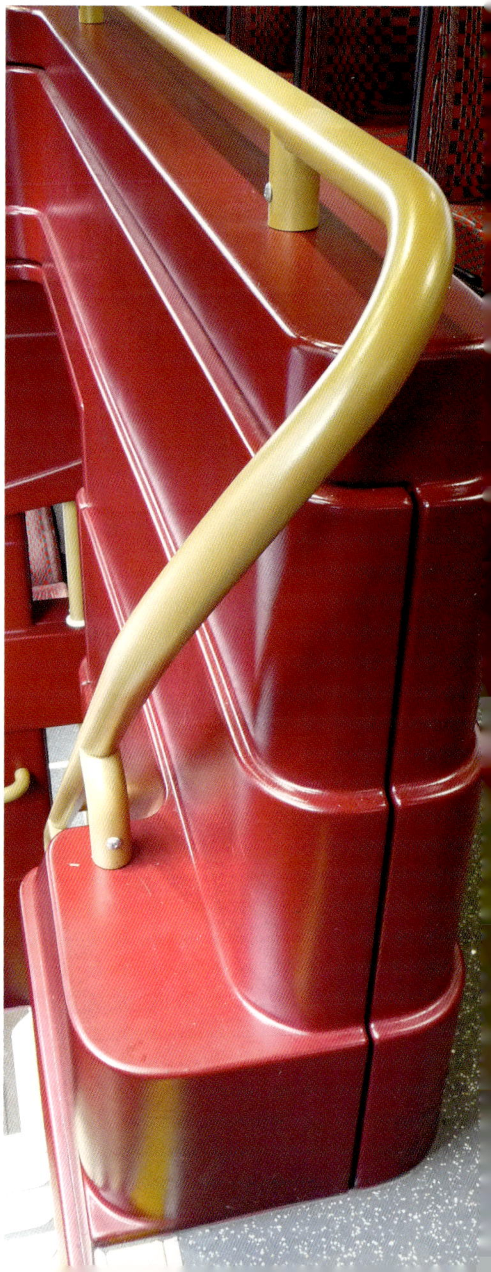

Attention to detail: a ceiling light, seat rail, burgundy Oyster card reader, wireless bell push integrated into a pole, and top of staircase.

A scale model of the rear section of the NBfL as exhibited at a special Heatherwick exhibition at the Victoria & Albert Museum in the summer of 2012.

Another small compromise was in the front upper deck window corner pillars. Passengers sitting by the side windows at the front find themselves looking straight ahead at a thick white pillar. This pillar was originally designed by Heatherwick to have been much thinner (see photo of the mock up of the upper deck on page 35). It was also a matter of some regret to the designers that so many vinyl stickers were needed. The utilitarian driver's mirrors half way along the lower deck interior (for the wheelchair space and the centre door) are other essential add-ons not designed by Heatherwick that detract to some extent from the overall appearance.

The seats may perhaps benefit from Heatherwick's studies in furniture design when he was at the RCA. The seat covering is a pleasing return to the colours used originally in the Routemaster but the pattern is very different. 'In the seat pattern,' says Heatherwick in an interview, 'we designed a repeat that was as big as the body. The distortion pattern is the same shape as your body, like contours of it.' In an interview for an exhibition held at the V&A between 31st May and 30th September 2012, Heatherwick gave some further details of their aims: 'The brief was never to remake something from the past, but we have not tried to reinvent ideas that don't need reinventing if there are things in the past that are useful. One of the most basic of these was the bus seats. At the moment when you get into a bus your eyes are bombarded with all these plastic bucket seats, and each one has a handle at the top of the seat and a crevice that a crisp packet can get caught in. We have reintroduced the bench seat with just one handrail across the top. All buses used to have that.' Two weeks after the V&A exhibition of the studio's work opened, Thomas Heatherwick spoke on Radio 4's *Today* programme: 'Dignity sounds quite a pompous word, but we were thinking about how we could reintroduce some of that feeling of the magic of travelling in a bus'. The studio seems to have succeeded.

MILLBROOK

HILTON HOLLOWAY

20th June 2011 was a day that the political opponents of London Mayor Boris Johnson had convinced themselves would never arrive. But on an overcast morning in Bedfordshire, I was one of a gathering of journalists at the giant Millbrook test track to view the first prototype of the 'New Bus for London' emerging from the distance. Johnson, standing on the vehicle's open platform, was understandably extra-bullish as the bus pulled up in the front of the assembled media. I was also rather wide-eyed because – as mentioned earlier in this book – I had visited Johnson in his campaign office in the old GLC building, back in early December 2007 with just such a proposal for a 'New Routemaster'. And here it was, a New Bus For London in its final form and, as we later saw, just a year away from entering service trials on the capital's streets.

To understand why Johnson's one-vehicle victory parade in Bedfordshire was such an important moment for him – after all this was a prototype of a new bus, not an attempt to put a man on Mars – it is necessary to remember how extraordinarily political his New Routemaster policy had been from the moment Johnson declared that he wanted to see a 'modern day' version of the Routemaster bus introduced to London.

I was fascinated by the Routemaster's structural integrity and refinement, compared to much newer buses. At worst, conventional rear-engined double-decker buses of the time seemed to be shaking themselves to pieces when idling, passengers being rattled by the big diesel engine seemingly trying to leap off its mounts. To me, these buses were also particularly noisy and unrefined, especially when pulling away from standstill. There seemed to be a serious lack of attention to what the car industry calls Noise, Vibration and Harshness. Recent bus designs have addressed this, but the NBfL goes further. Later, TfL boss Peter Hendy told me that the Routemaster's riveted aluminium monocoque structure was probably based on what the London Transport workshops had learnt from building Halifax bomber fuselages in World War 2. Perhaps it shouldn't have been a surprise that the Routemaster lasted so much longer on a London duty cycle that wore out more modern buses.

By a very handy coincidence Johnson's vision of an open platform was the perfect opening for adopting a non-mainstream hybrid transmission and one that is arguably more robust and easily repairable over the long term. This transmission uses electric motors to drive the rear wheels and the engine is used as a generator, feeding the electric motors and trickle charging the on-board battery, which accelerates the bus away from standstill without generating any pollution.

Explaining to the wider world why the NBfL was so different mechanically from nearly every other vehicle was very difficult. Although the design is labelled as a 'hybrid' – something most people recognise from automotive world – the bus is actually driven purely by electricity. The rear wheels are driven by electric

Opposite The test rig at Millbrook on 20th June 2011, when on display to the press. The rear offside corner panel covering the engine compartment is in fibreglass on the buses built for service. David Barnett has spoken about the work of containing the new technology within the bus: "This was one of the hardest challenges. We got the drive line hidden below staircases and if you walk through the vehicle you don't really know where that drive line is. You don't know where the main electricity centres are that control all of the various systems within the vehicle. That has been one of the big wins for us, as well as using 3D technology to enable us to redesign components to fit in with the aesthetic design."

New Bus for London
Development Vehicle
New Bus for London
Development Vehicle
WRIGHT

New Bus for London
Development Vehicle

motors, which are powered by both the bus's onboard battery pack and by a relatively small diesel engine (at just 4.5-litres in size, it is only twice the size of the diesel engine in the Range Rover Evoque). The diesel engine drives a generator, providing electricity for wheel motors.

The key difference between the NBfL's drive train and that used by conventional hybrids is that the NBfL's engine is not mechanically connected to the wheels, using only high-tension cables to transmit the electricity to the wheel motors. This set-up is known as a 'series hybrid' as opposed to the parallel hybrids, which have an electric motor sandwiched between the engine and gearbox. Arguably, the NBfL's arrangement has two crucial advantages for a hard-worked public service vehicle: first it is much less complex than a conventional hybrid. Secondly, this system uses a single gear ratio, the lack of gear changing making the ride smoother for passenger. Also, like the original Routemaster, the engine/generator can be removed relatively easily for replacement or repair.

Conventional buses have to have a rear-mounted engine, in order for the bus floor to be set low for easy access by passengers. In the original Routemaster, which had the engine at the front, the floor had to be raised high in order to clear the propshaft that ran under the bus, taking power to the rear wheels. With the series transmission, the engine/generator package could be neatly fitted in one corner (in this case, under the stairs), connected to the rear motors by heavy-duty cables, leaving the whole rear end of the bus open for the installation of a rear staircase and open rear platform.

Opposite The NBfL Development Vehicle, or test rig, was never intended to become a completed bus for passenger service. It was built solely for putting the design to the range of tests needed. Its front door is single leaf and hinged. It has no centre doors, just a fitment to give an impression of them.

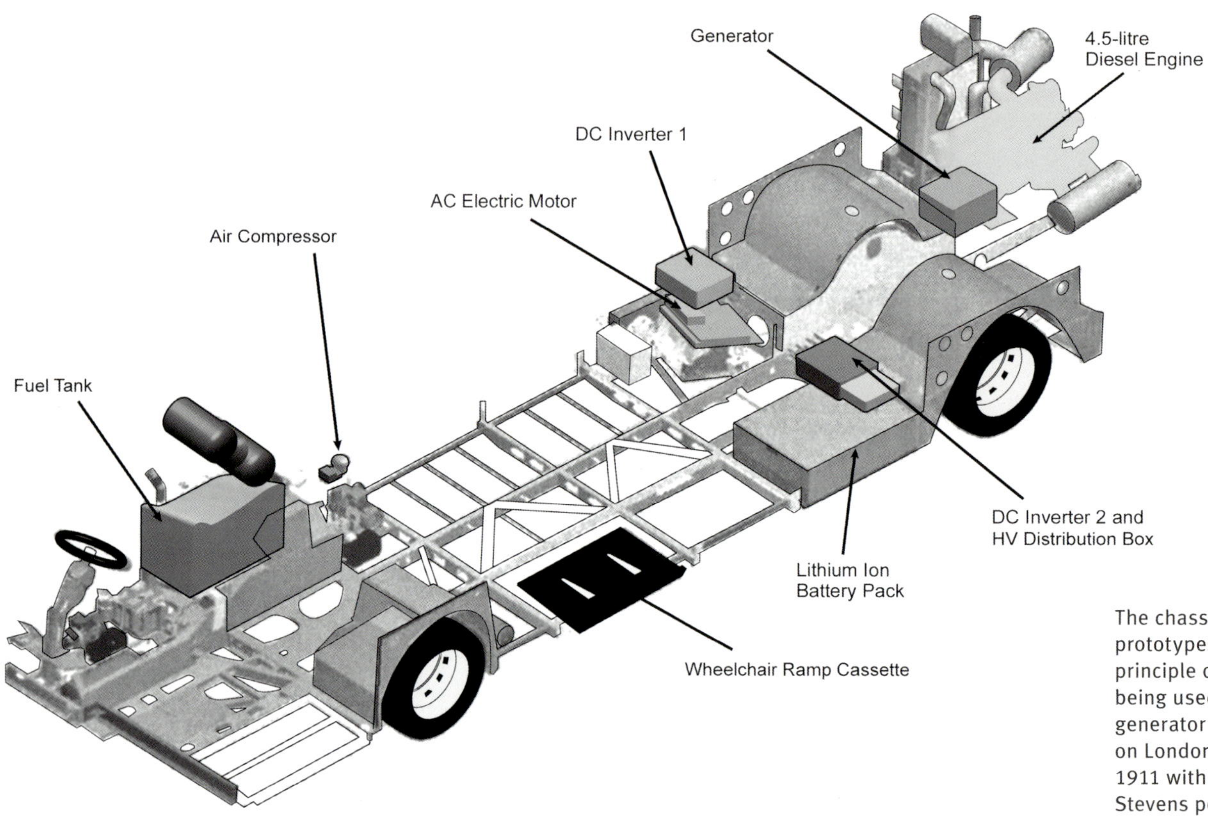

The chassis of the prototypes. The principle of an engine being used to drive a generator was first used on London buses in 1911 with the Tilling-Stevens petrol-electrics.

During the two years of development, the arguments about whether Mayor Johnson should be pursuing his policy of a bespoke bus for London continued to rage. Many of the exchanges, often deeply hostile, took place on the internet, particularly in the *Guardian*'s 'London Blog'. And many of the accusations were remarkably ill informed, such as the oft-repeated proposition that spending £11m on five (later eight) prototypes and the research and development needed for an entirely new kind of bus was a 'waste of money'.

Ask anybody in the car industry what an £11m investment would achieve, and the answer would probably be not much more than a set of new headlights and tail lamps. In stark contrast came the retorts that Transport for London, under Ken Livingstone, had spent £94m installing two lifts at Green Park tube station. Certainly, Britain's media and political elite are not over-endowed with engineers.

Boris speaks to the assembled press.

Below: Being unpainted, the vehicle showed the three different materials used for the exterior bodywork: aluminium, fibreglass (white) and Wright's composite material (maroon). The test rig continues in use for anything new to be tried out for the New Routemaster – or any other bus.

With his trademark overstatement, Johnson addressed the press pack at Millbrook and referred to the prototype's bare patchwork aluminium finish, comparing its appearance to that of the 1936 Supermarine Spitfire prototype. Despite appealing for recognition of the comparison from the assembled hacks, none came. I was probably the only other person at Millbrook who had seen the same pictures of the Spitfire prototype. Such knowledge of Britain's engineering achievements used to be a schoolboy staple.

As well as Johnson driving the bus for a short distance on the Millbrook apron, journalists were also allowed to experience a very short ride on the bus, again underlining that Johnson's vision had become reality. For those of an engineering bent, this prototype was especially fascinating because, for probably the first and last time, the guts of the New Bus for London were exposed.

Wrightbus's own aluminium spaceframe construction (a clever and efficient mix of simple aluminium extrusions and bolt-together joints) was on display inside the bus, as were the on-board electronic sensors, which were measuring every tiny deflection in the structure as this prototype was subjected to the Millbrook test regime.

Upper deck front and rear views showing measuring equipment installed in the test rig and Wright's Aluminique construction.

Although it wasn't readily apparent to the visiting press, the Millbrook test facility is enormous, taking in more than the high-speed bowl. Millbrook, among the many specific test areas, has three demanding Alpine-like hill routes, which are used to test braking, handling and transmissions. It also has a track course designed to simulate city driving and various rough and specially moulded road surfaces to check the amount of noise, vibration and harshness that is being transmitted into a vehicle.

'Twist humps' (a series of angled humps moulded into a tarmac roadway) are used to test the structural integrity of a vehicle. Finally, Millbrook also carries out the famous 'tilt test' where a bus is put on a tilting platform to ensure it can lean at precipitous angles before it will actually roll over. The NBfL prototype was put through all of these tests before the first five prototypes were released.

The NBfL Development Vehicle seen on the road near the Cummins factory in Darlington in September 2013. Some of the cabling fixed to it during its testing period can be seen in the rear view. The trade plate coincidentally carries the number of production buses ordered.

Perhaps most intriguing is Millbrook's all-important 'Drive Cycle' economy and emissions test. Developed by Millbrook and Transport for London, it is based on data from the real world 159 route, Marble Arch to Streatham Hill via Oxford Street. According to the detailed emissions testing information, the NBfL is the most economical 'Hybrid', beating the Wright's Gemini 2H by 11.6mpg to 10.2mpg. More importantly, in these tests the NBfL had the lowest Nitrogen Oxide and Hydrocarbon emissions of all its rivals.

Although my trip on the prototype was very brief indeed, most satisfying was the smoothness and relative silence of the electric drive train, as well as the promise of greater refinement promised by the unique construction technique. And, from a purely selfish point of view, it had the promise to attract cosseted car drivers like me to public transport.

Millbrook Emissions Testing

Vehicle	System	Euro	HC (g/km)	CO (g/km)	NOx (g/km)	Pm (g/km)	CO2 (g/km)	MPG
Diesels								
Scania	Diesel EGR	E4	0.049	0.090	11.546	0.130	1572.1	4.8
Wright Gemini 2	Diesel SCR	E5	0.028	1.985	7.734	0.053	1250.6	6.0
ADL Enviro400	Diesel SCR	E4	0.051	1.620	8.646	0.045	1253.1	5.9
Volvo B9TL / ADL	Diesel SCR	E4	0.000	0.013	8.583	0.030	1670.3	4.5
Hybrids								
New Bus for London	Siemens Series	E5	0.000	0.11	3.960	0.053	640.2	11.6
Wright Gemini 1H	Siemens Series	E4	0.012	0.039	7.616	0.060	866.0	8.6
Wright Gemini 2H	Siemens Series	E4	0.044	0.115	5.248	0.097	734.4	10.2
ADL Enviro400H	BAE Series	E4	0.053	0.815	8.792	0.029	856.1	8.7
Volvo	ISAM	E5 and EEV	0.020	0.152	6.738	0.043	937.3	8.0

THE LAUNCH AT WRIGHTBUS

GAVIN BOOTH

Launching a new bus to the media normally follows an established format – a gathering of the usual hacks from the trade press, a welcome from the managing director, a PowerPoint presentation by the sales director and then a chance to see, photograph, crawl over and even drive the new product.

The 4th November 2011 launch of the NBfL at the Wrightbus Ballymena plant was clearly going to be different. Normally the grapevine means we have a pretty good idea what we're going to see, but not in the case of the NBfL, and it was inevitable that there would be a much wider interest than normal in the new bus and so there were representatives from serious daily newspapers, radio and television stations, in addition to the familiar faces of the transport press.

One of the eight NBfL prototypes under construction at Wrightbus, Ballymena on the day of the November 2011 launch. From this angle, at this stage of construction, it does not look too different from conventional double-deckers.

There was a fair amount of stage management – and why not, after all this would be our first proper glimpse of a bus that had been talked about for some time, even by people who would not normally be interested in buses, and that had received more than its fair share of media coverage even before anybody had actually seen the real thing. And of course there was the Boris factor. We knew that London mayor, Boris Johnson, was going to launch the bus and we all knew that any event involving Boris would never be run of the mill.

At the appointed time the assembled hacks were ushered into the assembly shop where several more NBfLs were under construction, and while that gave us a clue about the shape and style of the bus we were about to see, they were still very much in the early stages of build.

After a wait, the roller shutters on an outside door started to rise and we got a first glimpse of the bus as it was driven into the shop. This, it was immediately clear, was a bus like no other. I can't recall if it got a round of applause but perhaps it should have done. What we were seeing had redefined the look of double-deck buses at a stroke, and its combination of bold styling with more than a nod to the past certainly ticked all the boxes.

From the rear the individual look of NBfL becomes clearer during construction, with the rounded rear dome in position and the aperture for the rear entrance very much in evidence. The composite rear end combines strength and weight saving. Any car that runs into the back of the bus is guaranteed to come off worse.

The wait is over as guests get their first glimpse of the NBfL at the Ballymena launch. Although a mock-up had been on view at the London Transport Museum, this was a first chance to see the real thing.

On the back platform was Boris Johnson, for the mainstream media possibly as much a star as the bus itself. He jumped off the platform to address the assembled crowd of local politicians, the Wrightbus staff who had worked on the development of the bus, TfL hierarchy and of course the media representing newspapers, magazines, radio and television.

'We've got this fantastic new bus,' he said, 'on which, amidst many other features, we've got the open platform back. We're going to bring that back to the streets of London – it was wrongly taken away. This is a world-class piece of technology built here in Ballymena. It's the most amazing futuristic design, but it's also the cleanest, greenest bus that will ply the streets of London, indeed any city in the UK.'

Johnson fielded the media questions as only he can – wittily but clearly demonstrating a knowledge of and commitment to the whole project. He spoke passionately about the bus, hailing it as a revolution in taste and design, and a great investment in London and British technology. 'The design will go round the world,' he said, 'influencing buses in London and elsewhere.' He continued: 'It's not just a bus, it's a visible statement of confidence in tough times and a reminder of TfL's role in driving jobs and investment throughout the UK.' He even referred back to the influence of Frank Pick in prewar London Transport, and Pick's statement that 'every bus should be a piece of street furniture', a view shared by Heatherwick Studio, which described the bus as 'moving architecture'. And Boris couldn't resist a dig at bendy buses 'threatening cyclists and belching out smoke like wounded bull elephants'. Then it was a chance to look inside to discover the innovative interior design, again a fusion of what seemed to be traditional ideas with modern materials and design concepts.

The retro look of the interior is attractive and welcoming, but on closer examination you realise just how much thought has gone into the layout, fittings and furnishings. The 'old-style' bus seats look very different to the modular seats fitted to most buses these days, yet when you use them you quickly appreciate the shaped seat back that helps to define 'your' half of the seat. And the deep cushions are an antidote to moves by some operators to cut back on seat cushioning, while the moquette has a traditional look without being in any way old-fashioned or a pastiche of earlier designs. Heatherwick Studio wanted to get away from the sometimes sterile effect of the fluorescent lighting in other buses, and came up with lighting that is subtle and effective, providing a balanced level of illumination at night.

There have been criticisms that the upper deck feels claustrophobic and it can seem this way, particularly to passengers used to the deep windows and arched roof of Gemini bodies. The upper deck windows on the LT are certainly shallower (at 24ins) than on the Gemini (35½ins) but they do afford an excellent view for seated passengers. The upper deck headroom is also less than on most other buses, though the headroom below the air cooling equipment and ducts on some Geminis is similar to the LT. It is in the rear section of the lower deck that headroom is a bit of a problem, being between two and three inches less than in the Gemini. Taller people need to take care when leaving the seats in this area.

Inside the assembly shop, guests had the chance of closely inspecting the bus inside and outside. The first drawings of the bus that had been released in May 2010 had been magnificently realised.

After our good look at the bus we were ushered outside to witness the sight of Boris Johnson driving the bus slowly out of the assembly shop into the November sunshine.

Thomas Heatherwick explained to me that his company had to learn about buses very quickly and he was able to question many of the long-accepted shibboleths of bus design. 'The bus had to look and feel good, but it also had to be comfortable', he said. 'The materials we used were led by the push to minimise energy use and keep weight down. Everything was designed from scratch – we didn't just take material from the parts bin and make it fit.

'From the outside, people will be able to see people moving around in the bus, as the glazing follows the passenger flow. We went for shallower windows upstairs to avoid problems of overheating in the summer, and nobody should need deep windows as they won't be standing. Travelling upstairs in a bus is a great experience, the cheapest high-quality view on the world.

'We wanted the lighting to be warm, and not the unflattering and uncalming fluorescent tubes that would be more at home in a piggery, so we are using low-energy LED lights. We are trying to reintroduce the 'specialness' of travelling by bus, taking into account all the rules, regulations and directives that have been introduced in the half-century since London last commissioned a bus for its streets.'

The specification of London's off-the-peg double-deckers has evolved and while passengers from other parts of the UK may find the interior layout unfamiliar to them, it is clearly what TfL deems necessary for London's apparently unique operating conditions. A separate exit door makes a great deal of sense in speeding up passenger flow, yet outside London even the most fervent advocates of two-door buses have reluctantly moved to a single door layout, usually citing the increase in the number of exit door accidents and insurance claims; a proportion of these are spurious, but the cost of dealing with these has driven most urban operators back to single doors.

At the time there was speculation about the long-term prospects of the NBfL. Would there ever be more than eight, we wondered. In conversation, Leon Daniels, TfL's Managing Director – Surface Transport, was being cagey, saying that as 'an old-fashioned bus person it is my view that the next job is to get thousands of miles on this prototype fleet before we take any further decisions on what happens next, because in the history of London buses over the last 100 years the ones that have been rigorously tested before going into production have lasted 50 years and represented very, very good value for the taxpayer and the ones that were rushed into production lasted five minutes and cost a huge amount of money'.

Leon's caution was understandable, and of course we know now that there will be at least 608 of them. It may not achieve the sales outside London that Boris was anticipating, at least not in London three-door form, but it looked to be well suited to London's needs, especially as the unit price of £330,000 that was being suggested at the 2011 launch has proved to be not too wide of the mark, and not significantly more than the cost of some high-spec hybrid double-deckers already in service in the UK. After the assembled media had finished with Boris Johnson he was whisked away to allow those of us who were left to explore the bus in more detail and to give Leon Daniels the chance he had probably been waiting for all day – a quick drive of the bus that TfL had financed.

LT1 poses at the Waterfront Hall in Belfast for one of its first publicity photos, its tree guard not yet fitted.

THE LAUNCH IN LONDON

JAMES WHITING

After its launch at Ballymena on 4th November 2011, the first New Bus for London spent some further time at the factory and was shipped over to England on 12th December ready for its London launch on the 16th. It arrived at Ash Grove garage on the 13th and on the following day it had its special exterior adverts and safety notices fitted and the Ibus vehicle location system commissioned. The 15th was set aside for training the driving instructors who would in turn be training the Ash Grove drivers selected to work on the bus when it entered passenger service.

The bus was carrying its newly selected classification of LT (a bow to London Transport) which had been decided on after the Ballymena launch. It replaced the even more prosaic HWP (Hybrid Wright Platform) that had previously been spoken of. It also carried a new registration number – L61AHT to L61HHT having been allocated to LTs 1–8. Although there had been some talk of a public competition to find a name for the bus, a decision had then been taken not to name it. This had not stopped quite a lot of names being suggested, many if not most ending with 'master'.

The big day was Friday 16th December. LT1 arrived at City Hall about 5.30am ready to be set up for a live LBC radio broadcast from 7am until 10. It was not the first time a bus had parked outside City Hall but it was not a common occurrence as the area around the GLA's headquarters is reserved for pedestrians and essential trade vehicles. The bus entered and left the area via Weavers Lane, which varies in width between 3.1 and 3.7 metres; special care was needed therefore and a couple of bollards had to be temporarily removed. LBC's live breakfast show was broadcast from the bus with an interview being included with Boris Johnson between 9.30 and 10, at the end of which LBC's engineers were given 15 minutes to remove all the broadcast equipment. And then Boris, keen to get behind the wheel again, drove the bus a short distance alongside City Hall until Leon Daniels took over the driving via Tooley Street and Stamford Street to Westminster Bridge for a photo shoot. From here Peter Hendy drove the bus to Trafalgar Square, the bus arriving for its launch about 11.15 with Boris on the platform.

With press photographers, and a few members of the public in the right place at the right time, taking their pictures, Boris Johnson waves from the platform of LT1, and shakes hands with an admirer, as it arrives at Trafalgar Square on 16th December.

LT1 is driven on to Trafalgar Square by Traffic Commissioner Peter Hendy with Boris Johnson on the platform.

Apart from the assembled press, the event also attracted passers-by intrigued by the new bus. Boris had been planning to make a speech from the rear platform, but got into the driver's seat again. After answering a few reporters' questions in the driver's seat he moved to the front platform. Here he gave his speech, which varied quite a lot from the speaking notes provided by his press office, showing again how very much he enjoys speaking off the cuff:

'Christmas has come early in the form of this revolutionary new bus whose gleaming coat of red paint and sinuous curves will brighten the day of all who see it humming along our great city's streets. It is the latest, greatest masterpiece of British engineering and design, and I am certain it will become a much loved and iconic vehicle akin to the legendary Routemaster from which it draws so much inspiration.

'It is, of course, complete coincidence that the first one runs past my house. It is a bus designed here in London, styled here in London, built in Britain. The bus has the domed look of the capital – St Paul's, a taxi, a bowler hat.' Referring to the Mercedes articulated buses that had been almost eliminated from London bus routes at the time of this launch he continued: 'Do bendy bus lovers want a British bus that is cleaner, greener, or a German-made bus unsuitable for British streets? I believe the approach we have taken will be copied. This is not a hop-on, hop-off you Frogs, two fingers to Europe, just a simple commonsensical approach to London's needs.'

Three key players in the NBfL story: Thomas Heatherwick, TfL Transport Commissioner Peter Hendy and London Surface Transport MD Leon Daniels.

Further opportunities for press interviews with Boris and with Peter Hendy then followed. The event was also shown on the lunch time news of both BBC television and ITV plus at least one overseas television channel. The bus remained on Trafalgar Square until after sunset so that more members of the public could have the opportunity to inspect it. It was incorrectly reported by the press at the time that the bus had a weight of 11,990kg, which was indeed close to the target weight (the mock up had displayed 11,800kg). LT1 and the rest of the prototypes actually weighed 12,650kg which was to have implications for the number of passengers that could legally be carried. The intended capacity of 87 was reduced to 78 in consequence when the buses entered service.

The moquette on LT1 was manufactured by Camira Fabrics in Austria, but this was deemed 'not to specification' by TfL and production was moved to the company's mill near Huddersfield. This increased the number of items on the bus that were made in the UK. The hybrid control system, electric motors and drive axle come from Germany, the doors from the Netherlands, curved glass from Italy and parts of the main flooring from France. The battery storage system is the only part to come from outside Europe; this is imported from China – a world leader in such systems.

Press and passers-by take a look at the new bus while parked on Trafalgar Square.

The day after the launch at Trafalgar Square, the bus was taken from Ash Grove garage to Stratford to be shown to shoppers visiting the recently opened Westfield shopping development, within sight of the new Olympic Park built for the following year's Olympic Games. As the bus was not allowed into the shopping centre, it was parked rather out of sight on Westfield Avenue, at the time a little used road, so many visitors to Stratford that day would have been unaware of its presence. On the 18th, the Sunday before Christmas, it went to Westfield White City and had a much more prominent position between Shepherd's Bush Underground station and the southern entrance to the shopping development. Here it attracted much interest and there was a high level of awareness among those who boarded it that it was 'Boris's Bus'. The majority of comments were favourable, as appears to have been the case wherever it was shown off, a common question being about when the buses were coming to the enquirer's route.

Its next public display was on 4th January when it visited Bexleyheath Broadway in the morning and Bromley High Street in the afternoon. This was followed by trips to Romford High Street and Ilford High Road on the 5th, Ealing Haven Green and Golders Green station bus layby on the 6th and Sutton High Street and Kingston Town Hall on the 7th.

The local newspaper for Golders Green reported that around 500 people had visited the bus during its stint there on the afternoon of the 6th. Students from a school in Harrow took a trip to the station to see it and a group of American tourists also took an interest. Finchley and Golders Green MP Mike Freer said the bus 'was sure to be a hit,' adding that he thought 'the new bus was excellent, modern, but with a clear echo of the original Routemaster'.

LT1 spent at least part of the next couple of weeks at Millbrook but was back in London for a 'preview ride' on the 23rd. *Telegraph* reporter Andrew Gilligan, later to become the mayor's cycling commissioner, gave the bus a mixed review: 'Although the buses will have conductors for most of the day, the conductor's role has deliberately been made close to pointless ... All this feels like TfL's sneaky bureaucracy (which never really wanted the bus) in action. By giving the conductors no real work to do, TfL is setting them up to be axed at the earliest possible moment ... Boris should put a stop to this transparent ploy. The conductors should sell tickets and swipe Oyster cards at people's seats.' He felt that the three doors led the buses open to bendy bus levels of fare evasion and that the conductors checking fares would pay for themselves in the revenue gained. This may or may not be the case, but the extra revenue would certainly go some way towards the cost and the other benefits of having a second staff member could certainly be argued as justifying the rest of the cost. Gilligan went on to say that he felt most people would love it. Comments from passers-by he spoke to included 'sleek', 'forward-looking' and 'classy'. 'Right down to its chunky bell pushes', he concluded his review, 'the Borismaster is thrillingly evocative of an age when form and function mattered in the public sector, when things were designed to please, to work, and to last.'

At the time of the London launch, no decision had been made about the staffing of the bus. What had been decided is that the second crew member would not collect fares and that his or her principal responsibility would be to ensure the safe boarding and alighting of passengers and providing assistance where needed. There had been some suggestion that these functions might be performed by a police community support officer. Leon Daniels, during his interview to become MD of TfL Surface Transport, was asked by Boris Johnson how he would staff the buses. Leon suggested out of work London actors as being people with the right type of outgoing personality and good knowledge of the capital. This idea was looked at, but considerations over the minimum wage ruled it out. The prototypes were in the event staffed initially by existing drivers doing driving and conducting duties alternately.

There was a last minute hitch with LT1, which meant it could not be the first New Bus for London in service as had been planned. A two-bus supplementary schedule for LT1 and LT2 had been published in February to start on 20th of that month, one of the LTs being shown as starting its duty at 0609 from Hackney and the other at 0657. In the week before the 20th, the date of commencement was put back to the 27th. Although it was later denied that it was ever the intention for LT1 to be in service on the first day, it had been announced on 24th December that LT1 would be in service within two months and then on 15th January that it would be on route 38 at the end of February.

LT2 was delivered the day before it started work, so its entry into service was somewhat rushed and the Arriva Licensing Clerk had to get to the Wimbledon DVLA office on the morning of the 27th so that the bus could start work at midday, rather than the early morning start that had been intended. It was not until 2nd April that LT1 was available for service and it was allocated to the 38 until 21st November 2012.

The weekend following the Friday launch at Trafalgar Square saw LT1 being shown off to shoppers at the large Westfield shopping centres at Stratford and White City. Then early in the new year the bus spent four days touring suburban shopping centres such as Kingston, where it is seen generating a fair amount of interest.

The launch and subsequent displays in London of LT1 enabled a closer look at the details that contributed to the bus's overall good looks. Above can be seen the recess under the stairs for the conductor. Frontal details are shown opposite and interior views on the following spread.

LT61 AHT
ARRIVA

VLT 14

Priority seats

Priority seats

ROAD TEST

MATT PRIOR

Public bodies have a tendency – understandably so, given that they're spending our money – to commission products on very specific and objective sets of factors. A jet fighter, for example, is measured by its ability to blow up other jet fighters; road signs are chosen for their clarity, not their beauty. Public procurement cares little for sentimentality. Here, however, is something different. Think of the NBfL as more like Heathrow's state-of-the-art Terminal 5 rather than the (barely) functional Terminal 3. NBfL's creators, Northern Ireland bus builder Wrightbus and design studio Heatherwick, have created a new London bus with a product that's almost as much about design flair as it is about transport. Almost. There's only so much you can do with a bus, after all.

Underneath its London Transport red skin lie the innovative bones of a novel product. The NBfL has a Wrightbus steel backbone chassis, to which is attached an aluminium superstructure and body. At 11.2m, the NBfL is a long bus, its length augmented by a composite rear section incorporating the rear stairwell. This also covers the generator (the NBfL is a series hybrid, more on which later) and, crucially, acts like a stiffener for the whole shebang.

If a supercar is dominated – and judged – by its engine, and a sports car by its handling, then a bus is absolutely defined by its interior. And nowhere on NBfL is the introduction of surprise and delight – so often a feature in today's cars but conspicuous by its absence in contemporary public transport – more prominent than inside. I don't think it's particularly controversial to suggest that, in general, bus interiors are ugly. It is cheap to fit a squared-off, plain rooflining and strip lights. It maximises interior space, too, but it looks desperately uninviting. By comparison, the NBfL is a triumph of interior design flair. The upper deck's ceiling has the gentle curve of a classic airliner's cabin, while LED soft-light pods cast a warmer, cosier glow than fluorescent tubes could ever hope to illuminate (yet are placed at each row to provide sufficient reading light).

If you've ever seen an urban double decker tottering along a motorway, you'll know that 'performance' doesn't mean the same thing to bus operators as it does to you and me. We didn't have time to strap our VBox timing gear to the NBfL during our test drive, but putting foot flat to floor at Nutts Corner circuit, near Wrightbus's Ballymena factory, revealed that the NBfL is capable of making only sedate, albeit sustained and linear, progress. Step-off from rest is decent enough; the 4.5-litre Cummins turbodiesel generator provides power to an air compressor (for the brakes and steering), a 75kWh battery and the Siemens electric motor, which lies beneath a raised seating area at the rear, from where it drives the back axle.

Left: The driver's seat is wide and flat, with great forward visibility.

In December 2011, to coincide with the launch of the new bus in London, *Autocar* magazine published a road test of LT1. This chapter is an edited version of that article. Matt Prior is at the wheel in this photo on the Nutts Corner circuit near Wrightbus's Ballymena factory.

It looks like there's quite a lot of lean, doesn't it? There isn't, not really. Or at least it doesn't feel like it from the driver's seat (upper-deck passengers might think differently). Thanks to a big overhang, you're aware that you're sitting way out in front, so it feels slightly precarious and you wouldn't barrel into a corner knowing you're among the first points of contact with anything coming the other way. But the bus steers moderately well and changes of direction are fuss-free. Will it drift? I imagine it would if it were on a frozen lake, but on a damp karting circuit in Northern Ireland I wasn't inclined to find out.

The electric motor does all the driving; the diesel generator is tuned to sit at optimum revs and provide all the power the batteries need, and it runs only when those batteries need topping up (which was most of the time during our test, although regenerative braking will assist on a proper bus route). The generator is overly grumbly during stop-start at the moment, but Wrightbus engineers are working on a fix. Braking is both by the drive motor and pneumatically assisted discs all round; retardation is fine and there's ABS, but pulling the NBfL to a rapid stop, perched as you are in front of, and mostly below, so much metal, isn't the most enjoyable thing you'll ever do in your life.

Here, then, is where we get to the nub of the *Autocar* road test: what's she like to drive? Seated in the widely adjustable but pretty flat driver's seat, you get a supremely clear view forward. The low-set steering wheel is very adjustable, so finding a comfortable driving position is a cinch, but the upright stance and wide chair mean it's more like sitting at a desk than in a car. The pedals are on the flat floor and the wheel is barely off the horizontal. Still, foot on the long-travel brake pedal, handbrake off and, as you ease off the pedal, the NBfL creeps forward with eerie smoothness. Never before has a hybrid drive train seemed so suited to a vehicle.

Fewer buttons are involved in driving the NBfL compared with other buses. The gear selector is the row of three buttons above the handbrake lever. The status of the bus is displayed on a digital panel in front of the driver (top right of the area within the steering wheel, enlarged in the picture below). This includes displays showing open doors, engine revs and the gear selected. Some small modifications were made to the dashboard when the production vehicles were built.

It's hard to gauge the ride across what amounts to a big kart track, but where the NBfL did meet imperfections, it ironed them out pretty admirably. On the road we'd expect the largely comfortable float you get in most buses, but with less of the accompanying crash over bigger potholes thanks to the composite rear end's body-stiffening properties. At 2.5 metres across, the NBfL takes up its share of road space, but its turning circle is superb at little more than twice the bus's length.

Nonetheless, if you haven't driven a cab-forward piece of kit before, it takes some getting used to: you turn the easy, slick and consistently light steering through its 4.5 turns later than you might think when exiting junctions, to give the ample sides room to clear apexes. But the NBfL's flat sides mean that its mirrors are supremely effective at letting its driver judge clipping points and gaps. Get into a groove and there's real pleasure to be had from driving the NBfL smoothly and placing it accurately – even more so because the power delivery is so smooth. The brake pedal could use a little more feel for our taste, though.

The NBfL won't be cheap in full-scale production, but neither are its competitors: other hybrid double-deck buses cost £300,000, and when you consider the 12 to 15-year lifespan in London, the NBfL doesn't seem like such bad value.

The bus at speed and nicely ironing out the bumps. All windows have bonded glazing for greater structural rigidity. The series hybrid system consists of a generator directly coupled to a small, efficient diesel engine, electric drive motor and high voltage battery pack. The engine and generator operate independently of the motor and driving axle, eliminating the need for a traditional gearbox.

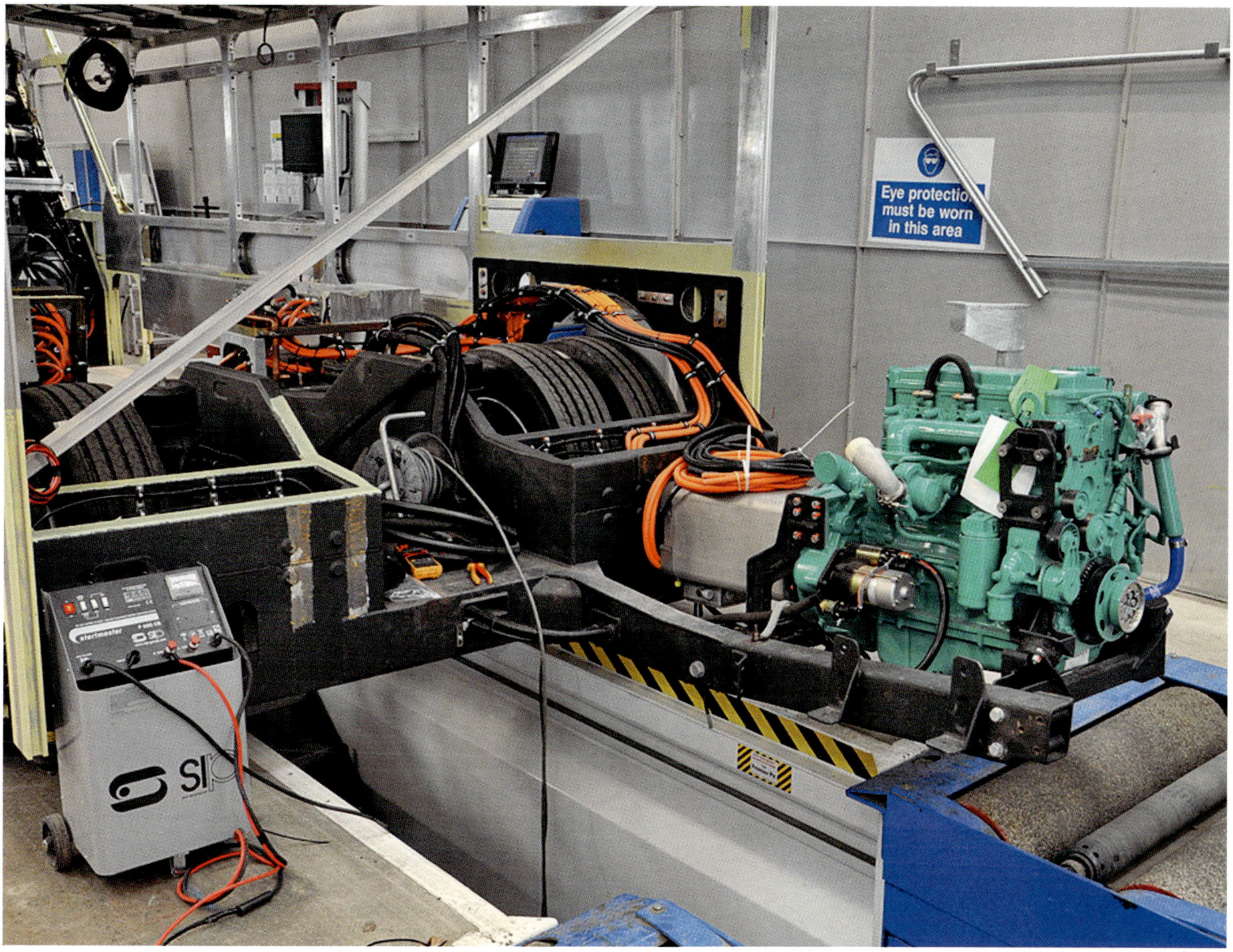

Some of Wrightbus's double-deckers use a Volvo platform, but the NBfL is all its own work. The basic load-bearing structure is a steel backbone, to which is applied the aluminium superstructure and body. As can clearly be seen in the picture above, the turbodiesel generator is slung off the back of the chassis on pontoon rails, making access easy. The rest of the hybrid power train is beneath the rear seats near the back axle. It's possible that the basic design could spawn single-decked variants or even an open-roofed double-decker, but it won't happen for a while.

The NBfL may lack the outright visual charm of the original Routemaster, but we're confident that our capital's first new bus for 50 years is as postcard-friendly as it's possible to get. More significantly, though, the NBfL is a triumph of product design in an otherwise utterly unengaging and unromantic market.

Travelling on one may not quite revive the joy of holidays by charabanc but, then, nostalgia's not what it used to be, and the NBfL is a darned sight more pleasant to ride on and be around than any other modern bus we've encountered. What seals the NBfL's five-star rating is that it's as advanced under the body as it is interesting inside it. Clean, efficient and thought-provoking: it's public transport as it should be.

The easy access turbodiesel generator, manufactured by Cummins in Darlington, is mounted well to the rear of the back axle (engines are now imported from the Cummins plant in Shanghai). Keen to avoid the fire problems that destroyed some Bendy Buses in service, a fire suppression system (not shown in this view) is fitted by Wrightbus above the engine. In 2014 TfL began to specify such systems for all new buses introduced on its route contracts.

THE PROTOTYPES AT WORK

JOHN ALDRIDGE

The first bus stop in Graham Road, Hackney is just round the corner from busy Mare Street with its numerous shops. For any bus that has terminated in Hackney and laid-over in Clapton bus garage it is the first stop for picking up passengers. By 11am on 27th February 2012 the shelter at the stop begins to attract those who know that the first passenger service journey by the New Bus for London is scheduled to leave from it at midday. All the seats of the shelter are soon occupied, one end filled by two mothers with young children in pushchairs. Most other waiting passengers stand between it and the bus stop post. Many of them are older men and several seem to know each other – more so than you would expect at the average bus stop. As each bus on the 38, 242 and 277 pulls up, few people board but the crowd goes on growing. Some of those waiting are plainly puzzled by the two mothers who totally ignore all the buses. It transpires that they are local, just heard about the new bus, and thought they'd like a ride.

LT2 slowly leaves Clapton garage with plenty of staff observing the event at midday on 27th February 2012. At Leon Daniels's initiative, the bus carries white on black destination blinds – marking the start of a fleetwide move back towards these and an end to the Dayglo ones.

Printed notice announcing the vacancies for conductors on route 38. The first line of the job description suggests that the conductor would not be confined to the platform for the whole of each journey, but this is largely what happened in practice except where a wheelchair user needed assistance. There was understandable concern initially that the new buses did not get the adverse publicity of someone being badly injured in a platform accident. On route 38 LTs, all the conductors were also drivers. Their work was equally spilt between driving and conducting. Keen to avoid the fire problems that destroyed some Bendy Buses in service, a fire suppression system is fitted by Wrightbus above the engine. In 2014 TfL began to specify such systems for all new buses introduced on its route contracts.

New Bus for London - Conductor

VACANCY

In February 2012 Arriva London will commence operation of the "New Bus for London", the first bus designed specifically for London's roads in more than fifty years.

This bus will operate with a crew of two drivers, one to drive the bus and the other to act as Conductor. Services will initially run from around 6am until around 8pm with a crew and then until midnight on a driver only basis, seven days a week. The bus will operate from Clapton/Ash Grove garage on route 38 and will initially operate in addition to the scheduled service although it will integrate into the full service in the future.

The role of Conductor is open to existing bus drivers and these staff will form a dedicated rota to operate the new buses.

Conductors will be required to:

- provide a supervisory / advisory role in respect of passenger activity on the bus, especially activity in the vicinity of the rear platform
- assist passengers in boarding / alighting as requested, particularly disabled passengers, or those with restricted mobility
- signal to the driver when boarding / alighting is complete
- providing passenger assistance and route, travel, fare and tourist information when safe to do so
- assist driver with the conversion of vehicle to / from crewed mode
- compile defect, quality or incident reports as requested
- complete fare validation checks as requested
- ensure their own working area remains Health & Safety compliant as well as exercising a duty of care to themselves and those around them in accordance with current legislation

Staff on the dedicated rota will work as both driver and as conductor interchangeably.

The successful applicants will be required to demonstrate strong customer service, communication and interpersonal skills and must be well presented at all times. Ideally, the candidates will have a good knowledge of London, both travel information and tourist information.

Staff who have been selected to work on the Olympic contracts will be excluded from this opportunity. Any staff who will transfer to other London Bus Operators under TUPE are also excluded.

Application Process
If you would like to be part of the NBfL team at Clapton/Ash Grove garage then submit an application on a staff memo to your Operating Manager by Saturday 10th March 2012. You will be required to undergo an assessment and interview process and your performance in your current role will form part of that assessment.

Arriva is committed to diversity. If you're good, you're welcome.

LT2 pulls onto the main roadway at the start of its first trip in service with a few people, mostly from the press and TfL, already on board. The advertising rights for the prototype LTs were retained by LBSL. For later buses, most of the advertising revenue went to the operators as with their own buses.

As noon approaches a bright red incident response van of London Buses draws up beyond the bus stop, as does a police car. A policeman appears and gently warns those standing on the kerb edge or in the road of the potential dangers and then leaves. They remain. Then a young woman in a high-viz jacket appears and shouts at them all to get back, but also leaves. Next, the driver of the van appears and tells those waiting that the bus has left the garage and is just out of sight round the corner. As LT2 hoves into sight he leaves. All three doors of the bus open and the crowd surges forward. Nobody could claim to be the first passenger!

LT2 at the first bus stop of its first journey in service. People began to arrive about an hour beforehand and by the time the bus arrived the number of people hoping to board it exceeded its capacity.

The bus entered service only a couple of months before the mayoral election for which the Transport Salaried Staff Association's preferred candidate was Ken Livingstone, who had said that if elected he would scrap the project. It seemed extremely strange for a trade union to be opposing a project which would increase the number of staff employed, but here a London Buses' Incident Reponse van tries to keep some distance between LT2 and the protest RML hired by the TSSA. Boriswatch, a web-based political blog, also kept an eye on the bus. In May 2013 it carried an article by the Green Party member of the London Assembly claiming that the prototypes in service were consuming twice as much fuel as claimed by mayoral press releases and that 'none of the hype about them being the greenest vehicles in Europe should be taken at face value'. There were certainly concerns about emissions and also a long delay in TfL releasing promised fuel consumption and emissions figures for the production batch.

Unusually too there is not a great rush upstairs to gain the front seats, but a surprising number of people head to the rearward facing seats downstairs – usually the last seats to be occupied on a busy bus. There are many more of these seats than on other double-deckers and the enthusiasts and experts in the know are keen to see how the open rear platform and rear staircase work in practice – not that this is in any sense a normal journey. The ladies with children made a beeline for the wheelchair space behind the front stairs. Not everybody at the stop was able to get on and one keen and fit young man sprinted off ahead, and was able to board a couple of stops later. There is an absolute jumble of people downstairs, standing in every available space, and boarding was inhibited by several tv cameramen with their tripods and soundmen with microphones.

Progress was slow, with long spells at stops while those trying to leave pick their way through the crowd. Other buses, including ordinary 38s, pass us. There is concern among the officials that while – as planned – the rear door remains open a loud warning buzzer sounds continually – which wasn't intended. There is a long stop at Islington station while the driver – an Arriva driving instructor – shuts down and then reboots the bus, with not much success. The software problem remains and it transpires the bus was only delivered to London the previous morning. Many passengers wrongly think the delay is caused by those wretched cameramen doing their interviews. One of them attempts to interview a child in one of the pushchairs. It promptly bursts into tears.

As the journey proceeds some impatient passengers leave, making way for others anxious to sample this bus. The ventilation system does not seem to be working properly and the upstairs windows have misted up. But people like the comfortable seats and the attractive interior. On battery drive the bus is impressively silent, but at the rear you can certainly hear the four-cylinder Cummins diesel engine, particularly when it first kicks in, with – like other hybrids – a rather agricultural noise.

As the bus approached many of the stops the rapid response van could be seen also. It was making spoiling moves to prevent a protest bus getting too close. A long Routemaster had been hired by the Transport Salaried Staffs Association, which was using it complete with large banners on the sides to protest about the new bus. Someone with a blond wig trying hard to look like Boris Johnson used a megaphone to shout the union's views.

En route a surprisingly large number of pedestrians spotted the bus and quickly took pictures of it on their mobile phones. The bus was a good 30 minutes late by the time it reached Victoria bus station, where a huge crowd awaited. They occupied not only the adjacent bus stands but a fair part of the roadway too. And there were no bus station personnel telling them off. Patiently, after unloading, the bus drove round to the offside of Vauxhall Bridge Road, where it joined other buses laying over. It received some electronic or mechanical attention from another red van, and was initially joined by that Routemaster again as pseudo Boris made another diatribe.

The Borismaster reappeared just before 3pm to return to Hackney, again fully loaded and again sometimes preceded and sometimes followed by the Routemaster with some more haranguing. This run was rather quicker, despite considerable traffic problems, and one further out-and-back run was completed later. Its first run had featured on lunch-time tv and radio, with inevitable descriptions of it as the new Routemaster. But no other bus ever, on its first day in trial service, can have had such a public start. It certainly contrasts with the first day of RM1 in service back in 1956. There had been newspaper stories about its debut, but public or even enthusiast interest was small and low key.

LT2 in Bloomsbury on its first journey in service. It was photographed and turned heads all along its route. Ash Grove garage was used for the prototypes because the LTs were a TfL project and Ash Grove is one of the very few garages owned by TfL. Crews came from Clapton garage in the morning and went back there at the end of their duty. The prototypes did not move to Clapton until 29th September 2014.

A large crowd greeted LT2 when it arrived at Victoria. In this view the bus is being driven for layover in Vauxhall Bridge Road.

Leaflets distributed by left-wing protesters, some of whom wore face masks, claimed that each bus cost £1.4m and that each passenger seated on board could instead have been bought a new BMW 3 series car. Similar claims that £11.4m had been spent on eight buses were made by opponents in news broadcasts. The protesters stand in front of LT2 while it is on layover in Vauxhall Bridge Road.

Passenger levels had become more normal for the second day's work for LT2. However, it usually ran only two or three of the five scheduled Monday to Friday round trips. Driver training and attention or checking by Wrightbus took up the rest of the days. The bus was driven by a driving instructor for the first few days, and then the standard procedure was for two drivers, one driving the other on the back platform alternately. They – and the LTs – were based at Arriva London's Ash Grove garage and provided a supplementary service that on paper was known as 38X and ran from Victoria to Hackney Central, just round the corner from Clapton garage, which was used for layovers. The normal 38 continued unchanged from Victoria to Clapton Pond, with about half the buses running only as far as Hackney Central and was worked from Clapton garage. For February and March LT2 was the solitary performer, LT1 having gone back to Wright's for modifications. It finally reappeared in London on 2nd April, and on Good Friday a few days later both buses were at work. But then gear-selection problems dogged LT1. When that was sorted it began what became quite a feature of life for some of the prototypes – visits to special events. LT1's began with the UK Coach Rally in Peterborough and the London Bus Museum's Spring Gathering at Wisley. Early June saw it in Wiltshire for the one day a year operation at the normally closed village of Imber.

Below: LT1 on Salisbury Plain in June 2012 as part of a special bus running event. The type has also visited the event, based on the military village of Imber, in subsequent years.

Opposite upper: LT1 visited the Guildhall in July 2012 for the Cart Marking Ceremony held each year in the city.

Opposite lower: LT3 on show at EuroBus Expo at the NEC Birmingham in November 2012.

Overleaf: Three prototypes spanning nearly 75 years at the 2012 London Bus Museum's spring gathering at Wisley.

Transport for London
ARRIVA
Designed for Londoners
LT61 AHT
hybrid

Designed for Londoners
cpt
ARRIVA

164A
MORDEN Stn UND
ST HELIER Av ANGEL HILL
HIGH ST SUTTON
BANSTEAD Rd SUTTON LANE
HIGH ST BANSTEAD
BOLTERS LANE BRIGHTON Rd
Keep Fit
Take Alka-Seltzer for Rheumatism
Keep Fit
Take Alka-Seltzer for Headache
2
SWISS COTTAGE
BAKER ST VICTORIA
VAUXHALL BRIXTON
HERNE HILL NORWOOD
CRYSTAL PALACE
London Transport Museum
One of London's best attractions at Covent Garden
www.ltmuseum.co.uk
EYK 396
SLT 56
RT1

Victoria
73
LT61 AHT
ndon Transport Mu
London's best attractions, at Covent Garde
Designed for Londoners

April 2012 had marked a turning point in securing the future of the class with the re-election of Boris Johnson as mayor of London for a second term. Official schedules for LT operation on the 38 had been available on the internet since before the start but at times were more a statement of hope. Next to arrive was LT6, which appeared in April, followed by LT4 in May. The buses were delivered in chassis number order, not fleet number order, hence the apparent out of sequence delivery. Originally the plans were for six operational prototypes, later changed to total eight. LT3 and LT5 were the last to be delivered in July, whereas LT7 had arrived in June, closely followed by LT8. A five-bus schedule had been introduced in June, at a time when there were only four LTs in the fleet! The schedule was for five buses on Mondays to Saturdays and four on Sundays. A seven-bus schedule was introduced from early August (7-5-3) and some days in October actually saw seven buses running. The reserved registrations for LTs 4-8 were not taken up, these receiving LT12 DHT to LT12 HHT.

From its earliest days the whole project attracted considerable media interest – and criticism. The most minor problems, such as the prototype running out of fuel on the Ml on a journey to the Millbrook test track, were adversely commented upon in a way experienced by no other bus type. The Green Party criticised the expense in a pseudo-calculation which assumed that London otherwise would not have needed to buy any new buses. Newspapers and tv news had plenty to say when a hot spell in summer 2012 saw high temperatures inside the buses: LT6 was returned to Ballymena for a month for tests and modifications.

The prototypes were delivered in order of chassis number and registered as shown:

001	LT1	2 April
002	LT2	27 Feb
003	LT6	23 April
004	LT4	23 May
005	LT7	28 June
006	LT8	4 July
007	LT3	8 July
008	LT5	12 July

This dusk view of LT1 at Victoria shows well the contrast in interior lighting between it and other London bus types. At Ash Grove, the buses soon developed a reputation for being less reliable than the Volvos. However, it has to be borne in mind that the new bus design, with its mix of tried and tested features and technical advances, was taken from concept to completion in a relatively short space of time. The number one priority was to have some running in service before the 2012 election.

Hackney Central
38
SCOTCH
STEAK
HOUSES
BRASSERIE
LT61 AHT

LT2 at Islington Green with conductor on board. It carried the special advert until July, when with the completion of delivery of all eight buses, the LTs received commercial advertising for West End shows. The advert reappeared on occasions when an LT was an exhibit at an event.

In contrast to criticism in the press and on television, most ordinary passengers liked the bus, the comfort of its seats and interior décor. Its greatly improved suspension was noted by some. On the pavements and roads its reception was remarkable with residents as well as tourists keen to photograph it. One middle-aged, middle-class woman with a loud voice boarded one with her female companion, explaining that the bus was going the wrong way for their intended journey but she thought they ought to have a ride on it. The buses proved attractive to advertisers with all eight carrying adverts for West End shows such as *The Phantom of the Opera* and *The Lion King*: toy maker Corgi even produced versions of its 1:76 scale models carrying these different adverts. The first motion picture to feature a Boris Bus was the James Bond *Skyfall*, released in the UK in October 2012, in which the rear of one of the prototypes, showing a 38 route blind, makes a fleeting appearance in a scene filmed in Whitehall. Further film exposure was given to the bus (this time using production vehicles LTs 10 and 95 showing 27 blinds) in *Paddington Bear*, filmed in 2013/14.

Early January 2013 saw the buses begin to be used on Monday to Friday evenings in one-person form. Visits to various events continued, including LT7 at the Goodwood Festival of Speed and its inclusion in the BBCtv programme *Top Gear*, a 10-minute feature including a test drive through some narrow country lanes by the programme's James May. It was not until June that operations of the six remaining prototypes were incorporated into the regular schedules, and permanently operated in one-person form. This was for just six buses, because by this time LT1 and LT2 had begun a joint world tour, beginning with LT1 in New York and Boston and LT2 in Europe; then in August LT3 went off to Hong Kong. Prototypes in London were reduced to four in October when LT8 was returned to Wrightbus in Ballymena for trial upgrading to Euro VI specifications. When it returned the following spring it became the first of the prototypes to change operating company, being allocated to Metroline.

A Corgi model of LT1 was issued in August 2012, followed by one, as part of a set, of the mock-up in September. Then, between February and August 2013 models of LTs 2-8 were issued, each with adverts for different musicals. All showed 38 Victoria as the destination.

FIRE DETECTOR
Fleetguard

Opposite: The Goodwood Festival of Speed event in 2013 provided an opportunity to inspect the engine compartment of LT7. The 4.5 litre Cummins ISBe turbocharged engine drives a generator providing electricity to the Siemens permanent magnet motor which drives the rear axle. The generator and motor are upgradable to keep pace with future advances in technology. The bus is also equipped with a 75kWh lithium-ion battery pack which sits under the rear floor ahead of the nearside rear wheel. This battery pack uses braking energy and stores it to help the NBfL pull away from rest without using the engine/generator.

Left: Beneath the higher stairs at the offside rear is the engine's radiator, equipped with four fans. The fuel tank is mounted towards the front of the bus, below the forward staircase. The fuel filler cap is behind a flap incorporated in a black panel that merges with the bus's glazing.

Below: The LTs on route 38, which had been running as extras since introduction, were integrated into the main schedule on 15th June 2013. One week later, they were converted to full one-person operation and the drivers that had been acting as conductors for part of their duty returned to full time driving.

TOURS ABROAD

ALAN MILLAR

During 2013 the UK government launched its Great Britain campaign to promote the country internationally as – in the words of the campaign – a great place to visit, study and do business. This was a multi-agency project involving the British Council, the Foreign & Commonwealth Office, UK Trade & Investment, the Cabinet Office, Department for Business, Innovation & Skills (BIS) and Visit Britain, along with selected private sector partners. As it travelled around the world, the campaign showcased readily recognisable uniquely British things. Like British Airways or traditional afternoon tea. Like a red London double-deck bus. And what better bus could there be than a New Bus for London to combine tradition with cutting-edge 21st century automotive technology?

Below Prince Harry and Prime Minister David Cameron leave the bus in Manhattan to take part in an event at New York's Milk Studios.

'What do you think of our bus?, asked Prime Minister Cameron when greeting the head of Milk Studios, where the PM was one of those speaking about the importance of the USA and the UK working together to promote trade in the face of increasing competition from Asia. 'I love the bus,' came the reply, 'I like the wrapround at the back'. LT1 is seen in the first view at Times Square and in the second view in use as a theatre during an internet week in New York.

So it was that with Wright Group as one of the campaign's private sector partners, first one and eventually three of the prototype Boris Buses were shipped off on separate legs or arms of this world promotional tour. LT1 was the first to go abroad, followed by LT2 and later by LT3. In so doing, they rolled into the ghostly tyre treads of London double-deckers – RTs, RTLs and Routemasters – selected for these sorts of promotional exercises in North America and Europe – at various points since the early 1950s. Like them, the 'New Routemasters' would act as magnets to attract passers by to come and find out more about why they should consider doing business with the UK. But this also was an opportunity for Wright Group to expose itself to a wider world, maybe – just maybe – to win export sales for this bus, but more likely to make potential international partners aware of its design and manufacturing expertise and the possibility of it building bespoke vehicles for new overseas customers.

Just like those earlier London bus tours abroad, there were logistical challenges to overcome. Shipping a double-decker across the world's great oceans is a task in itself, but that is only the beginning. Once on dry land, there are legal procedures to follow and in countries not equipped to accommodate 14ft 5in high vehicles, there are obstacles to negotiate – not just the immediately obvious ones like bridge clearances and overhead wires, but the things like traffic lights and direction signs that sometimes hang below these wires. Or narrow mountain roads with steep drops when moving the buses between venues.

The campaign launched in New York on 14th May 2013, with Prince Harry and prime minister David Cameron arriving aboard the back platform of LT1. Their presence demanded high levels of security and secrecy. The bus was already on the high seas to America before word began to be put out that it was anywhere other than in London or Ballymena. It arrived five days before the launch, and was met by a London bus driver qualified and experienced to handle it. Only this was where officialdom began to exert its influence. The New York authorities

The bus stood out among New York traffic and required special manouevring in places.

required that its movements on the public highway of Manhattan should only be in the hands of a United States-licensed driver. The Metropolitan Transportation Authority duly found one, someone it assured the UK delegation was one of its best – possibly even the best – man for the job. There were however the small details that he had never previously driven a double-decker bus, nor any kind of right-hand-drive vehicle or a hybrid electric. He had his own learning to do.

On the move, the bus was accompanied by a police escort and the roads were cleared as necessary to let it progress. The comments of taxi drivers and delivery van drivers can be imagined. And all this involved making zigzag movements around traffic intersections, to keep the bus clear of those hanging obstructions.

LT1's driver in New York and Boston was local man George Denning, in a uniform flown over with Leon Daniels's luggage that may have convinced locals that London bus drivers were to be seen in it. With Mr Denning are MP Nick De Bois and Consul General Susie Kitchens.

LT1 crosses Charles River by traversing Harvard Bridge with a party of sightseers.

The bus then went to Boston, where it arrived on 29th May 'with full fanfare' according to a local report. Here it was scheduled to stop at every UK brand outlet in upmarket Newbury Street to celebrate all things British – and so it did, except one. Burberry's at one end of the street had to be skipped because First Lady Michelle Obama was campaigning next door for a Senate candidate – though surely she would have liked to see it! Support for the city following its terrorist bombings earlier in the year came by the bus visiting the site of the bombing.

LT1 climbing through the Andes on its way to Bogota. It was beautiful scenery for the team on board, but coupled with very demanding driving conditions at times.

After Boston the bus was sent again on the high seas to Colombia, in the north-western corner of South America. Its port of disembarkation was Cartagena, on the Caribbean Sea coast, but there were five cities to visit including the capital, Bogotá, and Cali in the south-west, where the World Games were being staged. By comparison with what would follow, the visits to the northern coastal cities of Cartagena, Baranquila and Santa Marta were child's play. Perhaps the journey to Bogotá was the biggest endurance test the new bus had faced since its conception. It is arguably as testing as the torture inflicted on the development rig at Millbrook.

Bogotá itself is 8,600ft above sea level, with air quality quite different from that experienced in London, but the overland route scales much greater altitudes. At its highest, the road through the Andes is 10,500ft above the oceans and this is no North Circular or M25. There are stretches with steep cliffs to one side, sheer drops to the other. There are bridges and other sections little more than a hair's breadth wider than the 2.55m of LT1. Locals told the team that they were sometimes driving where even the seemingly daredevil lorries did not go. The bus travelled with a kit of all the obvious spare parts it might be expected to need, but one wrong move and £300,000 of capital asset could plunge into oblivion.

While the responsibility of keeping the bus intact may have induced the odd sleepness night, the rewards for the team taking care of it were to admire the stunning scenery and enjoy the warm welcome this bus – unusual to their eyes – received from the Colombian public. Corey Link, the Wrightbus service engineer who accompanied it from New York to Colombia's Pacific coast, talks of it taking people by surprise and putting smiles on their faces. 'Often vehicles would overtake the bus, only to be pulled over 5 miles up the road with occupants out of the vehicle, standing with cameras ready as we came driving by again.'

The same kind of thing happened when it was taking part in any of the static displays in cities as part of the Great Britain campaign. They showed great patience in participating in another great British tradition, the queue, waiting in long lines for their turn to board and see inside the bus. They also wanted to photograph the bus and be photographed with it and some of the people taking it around this part of the world. Not that what they found inside LT1 was entirely what a London bus passenger would discover. Some of the seats had been removed to display travelling exhibits and behind the front windscreen upstairs was a 47in LCD flat screen television monitor to show promotional films. It was to conceal that screen that the GREAT logo was displayed at the front.

For its week in Bogotá, LT1 was stabled on the premises of TransMilenio, the city's rapid transit bus operator. The New Routemaster may not fit into any of its future plans, but the manufacturer and operator both now know a lot more about each other's capabilities. Between there and Cali, it visited the city of Medellin.

After Colombia, LT1 went on to Asia, first to South Korea, then Malaysia (including the capital Kuala Lumpur) and then to Bahrain in January to coincide with an air show there. These all are territories where Wright Group is keen to develop new partnerships as part of its drive to derive at least half of its business from markets beyond the UK. This was especially true in Malaysia where it showed the bus to a couple of dozen potential bodybuilding partners. In South Korea, it was used as a temporary classroom for part of the GREAT campaign and undertook a series of tours of the capital city Seoul, one of them with a group of defectors from North Korea. Having already encountered a prince and a prime minister at the start of the campaign, while in Korea it met with a senior cabinet minister when William Hague – then foreign secretary – while he attended an international conference there.

Its work complete in Bahrain, LT1 went on to Masdar City, Abu Dhabi where it transported guests on 10 June 2014 at the official opening of a permanent office there for Wrightbus International. It remained in store there pending a decision on funding for an extension to the Great campaign. India – where Wrightbus is involved in a joint venture with Mercedes-Benz owner Daimler Buses – remains a potential destination for future tours.

LT1 outside the large Avenue K shopping mall in the centre of Kuala Lumpur. Just visible on the right is a Union Jack painted mini that accompanied the bus here.

It became necessary to have more than one bus for the campaign, as the various agencies involved began to arrange visits to widely scattered cities, countries and continents on dates that would have clashed had only one bus been available. Not every GREAT visit required a bus, though, nor could one always be accommodated, especially where the domestic agencies on the ground put a complete block on the movement of any vehicle more than 4m high. A New Routemaster is 4.4m high. Sometimes the British embassies hosting the exhibitions knew their way around the bureaucracy, but other times it required bus experts to explain what they wanted to achieve. Shifting a bus around Europe was sometimes more procedurally difficult than those hair-raising overland drives through the Andes. It never got to Germany, nor could it travel across it, so a boat trip was needed between Holland (where it was not exhibited) and Poland.

The bus selected for the European tour was LT2, which had been the first New Routemaster in public service in 2012. It was adapted to a similar standard as LT1, but stripped of its upper deck seats, and visited Brussels and Leuven in Belgium, Poland, Austria, Hungary, Serbia, Bulgaria and Turkey, from where it returned to England by boat. The two views here show it in Brussels where the local pop radio station, Radio X, teamed up to provide a band to play on the bus.

While touring Austria in October 2013, LT2 first visited the Lentos Kunstmuseum in Linz to publicise a forthcoming exhibition of British art from the 1970s. It was also put on display at the United Nations centre in Vienna before moving to the city's Kunsthistorisches Museum to promote a Lucian Freud exhibition, where a group of students display some interest.

The campaign had moved on to Hong Kong in October 2013 and with LT1 already required elsewhere in Asia this was the moment to conscript a third bus into the world tour. LT3, without the big screen television upstairs, but otherwise similarly attired to the other two, was selected for this and a subsequent visit to Singapore – both of them key export markets for Wrightbus double-deckers. In Hong Kong, the bus was stabled with the largest operator, Kowloon Motor Bus, which provided a driver to move it around.

Among the many facts of life about this former British territory is that it has one of the most active and youthful bus enthusiast movements. Last days in service by what older British enthusiasts might regard as rather ordinary and at best mildly charismatic buses attract crowds of bus fans of a scale that would impress travelling rock stars. There also is a vibrant collectors' market for models of modern buses. Knowing some of this, the Wright Group people thought they would try and keep its arrival under wraps by moving it between the docks – where it was offloaded from a shipping container by giant forklift truck – and the KMB depot under the cloak of late evening darkness. That may have been the plan, but around a dozen enthusiasts were waiting outside the dock gates and followed the bus in their cars, photographing almost every move every inch of the way. The night staff at KMB were just as enthusiastic, descending on LT3 as soon as it reached the depot, eager to have a good look inside and be photographed behind the wheel.

LT3 arrives in Hong Kong and is moved to KMB's premises after dark. It had in any case suffered some delay getting off the boat.

Locals point their camera phones at LT3 in Hong Kong.

All this was a dress rehearsal for the media feeding frenzy that would accompany the bus once the official GREAT events took it around parts of Hong Kong. The senior British politician for this leg of the tour was Mayor of London Boris Johnson, the man who had made the development of a New Routemaster part of his election campaigns. As one of the most colourful – and ambitious – figures in contemporary British politics, he clearly was the main attraction on the day, but the Boris Bus (accompanied by a couple of Boris Bikes) was a huge draw for the Hong Kong public, especially in the moments when the mayor and his entourage were breezing off somewhere else.

LT3 on display in Hong Kong along with a British Airways Airbus A380 airliner.

LT3 on display in the West Kowloon Cultural District, against a backdrop of Victoria Harbour. Alongside are a Daimler double decker of a type that ran in Hong Kong from 1949 to the 1980s and an Albion single decker.

Kowloon Motor Bus's corporate affairs director, Vivien Chan, said 'While KMB has no intention of introducing the NBfL to Hong Kong in view of the lack of air-conditioning and the open design of the rear door, we have incorporated some of the environment-friendly features as well as the ergonomic seat design on newer buses in our fleet'.

From Hong Kong, LT3 was shipped to Singapore for the month of February 2014, with key Wrightbus customer SBS Transit accommodating it at its Hougang bus depot for the duration. One notable change there was to the fleetname. All three had toured the world thus far with the Arriva fleetnames they had carried while operating route 38 in London. But SBS Transit is the home fleet of global transport giant ComfortDelGro, whose London subsidiary is Metroline and it gained Metroline names for its Singapore stay. While there it visited Suntec City – a downtown equivalent of London Docklands – and the adjacent Conrad Centennial Singapore hotel, and *The Straits Times* newspaper quoted one impressed enthusiast saying after a demonstration ride that 'it is more comfortable than our double-deckers here'.

Singapore was the first country in the world to introduce a congestion charge, which it did in 1998. LT3 is seen about to enter the Electronic Road Pricing zone and also within the zone with its many skyscrapers. With Metroline being a Singapore-owned company, its fleetnames replaced Arriva ones on LT3.

Hop on the new London bus

It's big, red, and a real head-turner. You can now catch the iconic London bus – or the new Routemaster – right here in Singapore, as part of a month-long tour to promote Britain.

8 facts about the new London bus

1. Inspired by the old Routemaster, a well-loved London icon, which was retired in 2005.

2. It is the first bus in more than 50 years to be designed specifically for the streets of London. It began service in 2012, and more than 600 of them will ply the streets by 2016.

3. Designed by celebrated British designer Thomas Heatherwick, the brain behind the Olympic cauldron for the London 2012 Games.

4. The red double-decker retains the "hop-on hop-off" rear-open platform – a distinctive feature of the original Routemaster. But the platform can be closed when not needed.

5. The bus, which is 11.2m long and 4.4m tall, can take up to 87 people.

6. It has three doors and two staircases. The bus also uses the latest diesel-electric hybrid technology.

7. Each bus costs about £354,500, compared to about £326,000 for a standard bus.

8. Two original Routemasters are still in use today on heritage routes in London.

Where to catch the bus

• It will be here until the end of February as part of a world tour to promote Britain. Earlier stops on the tour included the United States, Hong Kong and Malaysia.

• You can still catch the double-decker at the following locations:

Wednesday, Feb 12, 2014

Rainbow Centre Singapore
51 Margaret Drive
9.30am - 10.30am
2.00pm - 3.00pm

Sunday, Feb 16, 2014

One° 15 Marina Club
01-01, 11 Cove Drive, Sentosa
At the Clipper Race
10am - noon

Gardens by the Bay
(Marc Quinn's Planet sculpture)
4pm - 6pm

Source: Transport for London, British High Commission Singapore

For more information, go to **www.facebook.com/UKinSG**

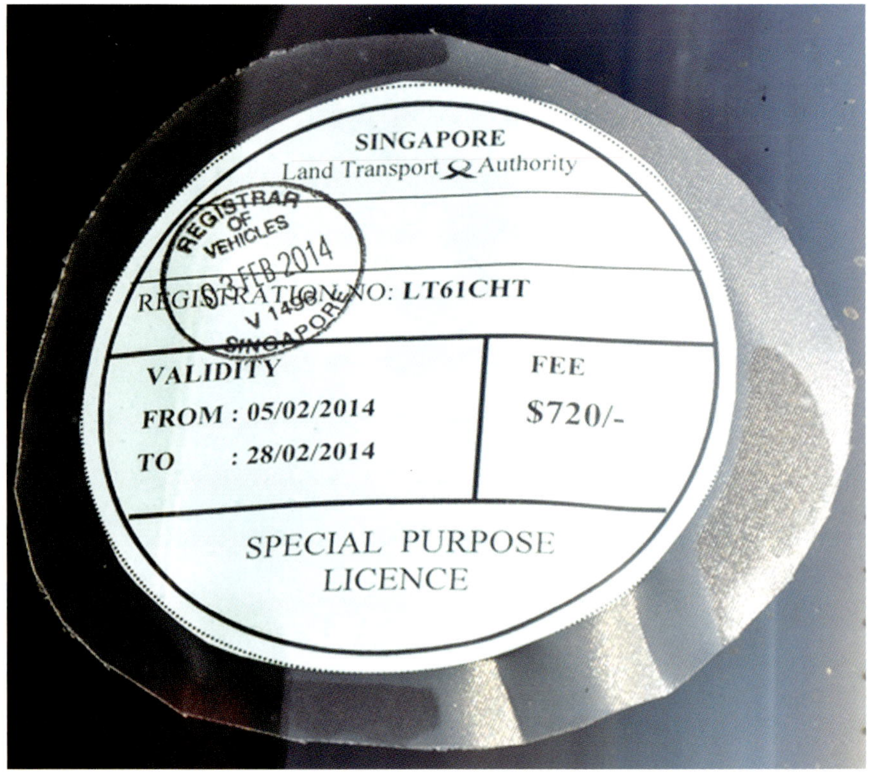

Opposite: Advertising for the displays of the bus in Singapore, its local special purpose licence and the bus at the Marina Club.

This page: These photos show LT3 at Gilman Barracks, Singapore, on the occasion of an on-board art exhibition. The placards refer to a photo competition for views of the bus on its tour of the country. Two air-conditioning units and two fans were used inside the bus while the exhibition was on. The yellow tubes are for the air conditioning.

THE BUS IN PRODUCTION

JAMES WHITING

Following the completion of delivery, in July 2012, of the eight prototypes and re-election of Boris Johnson, an order was placed with Wrightbus in September 2012 for 600 further LTs. Approval for this was given by the TfL board on the 20th. It was anticipated that the first batch of 30 buses would enter service by the end of the following April, though at the time the first route to have the production vehicles had not been finalised. As part of the contract between Wrights and TfL, which envisaged 127 LTs being delivered in 2013, 270 in 2014, 184 in 2015 and 19 in 2016, another 400 needed to be ordered before another manufacturer could be invited to tender.

The nice touch, at Hendy's initiative, of Northern Ireland registration numbers to accord with the fleet numbers of the buses gives a clue to the size of the fleet he would like to see, for he requested the reservation of 3,000 marks for 3,000 LTs. This was refused by the DVLA in Belfast but it did allocate matching numbers to cover the eight prototypes and the 600 then on order. Whether the buses would ever be bought by service contractors to TfL rather than TfL itself remained in question at the time of the November 2014 order for another 200 buses.

In a break from the system that had been in place since route tendering began, the buses would be owned by Transport for London and supplied to the operating companies on a notional lease. It was almost inevitable that this would be the case for a number of reasons. Commercial leasing companies had come off badly from the early withdrawal of the bendy buses and the difficulty in finding new customers for them (some ended up in Malta, where engine fires were again to be a problem). Undoubtedly then, their leasing charges for a bus that no-one else in the UK was likely to want would have been high. The bus operators would be unwilling to be responsible for a new bus that their engineers had not specified nor for the financial penalties that would apply for buses being out of service for mechanical reasons. TfL owning the buses was realistically the only option.

It was an arrangement which, though initially a large financial burden on TfL of over £200m, was expected to save money in the long term. It would also enable the buses to be easily moved between operators as route contracts changed. The leases contain clauses to ensure that the LTs are maintained to a standard that would not place obstacles to this. Such a move would be unnoticed by most passengers, as the conductors would move also. Maintenance of the buses is the responsibility of the operating companies, which are however able to subcontract the work to Wrightbus at a TfL-negotiated price as is provided for in TfL's contract with that company. The contract specifies that spare parts for the buses will be available for 29 years (ie until 2045 in respect of the order for 600), made up of 14 years of anticipated service in London and 15 years thereafter. Annual mileage for each bus is assumed to be 56,000.

LT17 has been brought from Ballymena to pose for the official opening on 10th May 2013 of Wright's new chassis plant in Antrim, which began producing chassis for the new bus in April 2013, that for LT32 being the first. LT17 carries the registration intended for LT1 for the occasion. Outside, further completed buses are lined up for the photographers present. The matching registration numbers on the production LTs certainly make identification of the buses easier for staff.

Production of the 600 LTs began at Ballymena around the time the contract was placed and in April 2013, when the first buses left the factory, it was announced that route 24 would be the first to receive the buses, on which they would enter service on 22nd June. Twenty-seven buses would be allocated to Holloway garage plus five spares. The aim was to convert at least two and possibly three routes in 2013, ruling out a full conversion of the 38, the 73 or indeed any other routes needing more than 30-35 buses. A number of routes in this category were considered and surveyed in spring 2013, including the 9, 11, 19, 23, 24, 88, 94, 168, 189 and 390. Among the other factors governing the choice of the earliest services for the buses was the desire for them to be visible in many different parts of central London. In the event four routes were selected to receive LTs before the end of 2013, the 24, 11, 9 and 390 in that order.

This page and opposite: An NBfL chassis being assembled at the EN-Drive factory in Antrim, with the Cummins engine mounted in-line in the offside rear. Once completed, it was transported by low-loader to the bodybuilding plant in Ballymena. Forward of the rear axle, the chassis is largely identical to that of the StreetDeck announced towards the end of 2013. Besides the NBfL, the EN-Drive factory also assembles the StreetLite single-deck chassis with low-entry body and centrally-mounted rear engine.

AH818

AH819

Brent Cross 326
Metroline
LK08 DWX
Metroline
LT16
hybrid
LK13 FJN

Metroline
Transport for London
hybrid
LK13 FJN

The selection and the training of staff to be conductors on the buses were the responsibility of the operator. The contracts were amended so that the total cost of training and employing the extra staff member was covered by TfL. Pay with Metroline was £9.30 per hour basic, £9.80 for weekend work and £10 per hour for overtime. Training of conductors (or customer assistants) for the 24 was carried out by Metroline at Cricklewood garage and on the route over a three-week period ending on 21st June. The training included trips along the route in a bus with other conductors to learn about places of interest and gain some familiarity with the bus stops. It was also important to be fully familiar with those controls on the bus that the conductors would be responsible for, the types of question they might be asked and the handling of passengers in wheelchairs.

Successful applicants would be those with good customer service skills (exemplified by the volunteers at the previous year's Olympic Games), a good knowledge of Underground and bus routes and very good spoken and written English. The great majority of appointments for the 24 were full time, with four part-time staff. During the week before the route was converted to LTs, the buses destined for Holloway garage were assembled at Perivale ready to be driven to the garage on the evening of the 21st. The following day, after a gap of 7½ years, two-person operated buses would be running in normal service on a London route.

The drivers, each of whom was given 12 hours familiarisation on the new bus, have ultimate responsibility for the safety of passengers. The conductor's main job is to safeguard passengers boarding and alighting at the rear platform. The conductor signals to the driver that the rear platform is clear and the bus's handbrake is not released until this signal is given. As on conventional buses, the driver is responsible for checking the centre doors by means of ceiling mounted mirrors in the saloon and cctv in the cab. The public address is also in his charge.

CUSTOMER ASSISTANTS

Are you a unique performer? Do you have the ability to play to an audience? Do you really care about the customer experience? Do you want to be involved in a unique opportunity in Central London?

Metroline will be showcasing to the world when its route 24 becomes the first route in London to be converted to the New Bus for London.

We are looking for unique people that can become the life and soul of the route 24 as it travels through some of the most magnificent sites in London.

Full and part time vacancies available. In your written application, please tell us about your availability. Games maker qualities are essential!

Responsibilities will include:

- Providing general customer assistance with route, travel and tourist information.
- Providing assistance to wheelchair and buggy users
- Providing a visible presence in the vehicle to customers
- Ensuring customers board and alight the vehicle in safety.

Opposite top: The first production LT to arrive for route 24 drives into Cricklewood garage yard on the morning of 16th May 2013, where it will be used for training purposes before moving to Holloway garage. Cricklewood's routes 16, 189 and 390 were also on the blinds of the batch delivered for the 24, suggesting future intentions at the time. TfL specified that the fleetnames were to be in white and the Comfort DelGro lettering below Metroline was white on later deliveries. The allocation of Northern Irish registrations came too late for the first four production LTs to be delivered:
LT10 (LK13FLE),
LT11 (LK13FJJ),
LT12 (LK13FJF),
LT16 (LK13FJN).
All four were re-registered later.

Opposite bottom: Another view of LT16 at the same location during the training of customer assistants for the 24. Training was spread over three weeks, split between classroom and on the road.

Left: Part of the advert for conductor jobs on route 24. With this conversion, the official terminology for the second crew member changed to 'customer assistant' to reflect the fact that they did not collect fares. This did not stop most people referring to them as conductors.

On Thursday 20th June, the LTs for route 24 are lined up ready at Perivale and are having their exterior adverts fitted. The following night they will be driven to Holloway ready for service on the Saturday. LT15 was delivered carrying the registration number for LT22, which LT22 also carried. This was corrected before the buses entered service.

Pimlico 24
LT24
LTZ 1024
LTZ 1037
LTZ 1015

LTs on the 24 did not get off to a good start on 22nd June 2013. In the weeks preceding, a house to house delivery of 141,000 eight-page fold out postcards was undertaken at a cost of £30,000 to sing the praises of the new bus. In theory there was much to be praised, but in practice the service provided in the first few days was a substantial drop in quality compared with the service the people along the route had been receiving with the buses previously used.

As the 24 route operates 24 hours a day the first LT journey from Hampstead Heath coincided with the transition from opo to crew operation and left on time at 6.56am, driven by Surface Transport Managing Director Leon Daniels, arriving at Pimlico about 25 minutes late and back at Hampstead Heath at the end of the first round trip almost an hour late. The main cause of delays seems to have been the unfamiliarity of passengers with the boarding and alighting arrangements at bus stops, but road works in Victoria Street also contributed. This late running was to continue all through the day with drivers recording serious delays, leading to curtailed journeys. It probably did not help that the Northern Line paralleling the 24 was closed for engineering works that weekend. A few of the buses had problems with the door alarm systems (as had been the case with the very first LT journey on route 38) and there were a number of other breakdowns. Extended intervals and bunching were therefore inevitable.

A number of VIPs were present for the first journey, the bus selected for this honour being LT32. Apart from Leon Daniels in the driving seat for the first trip, Metroline's CEO Jaspal Singh, its Chief Operating Officer Sean O'Shea and Holloway garage's chief engineer were joined by Mike Weston (Buses Director of TfL Surface Transport) at Holloway garage for the bus to make its way to the Hampstead Heath terminus for its first trip to Pimlico. Sir Peter Hendy (knighted in the New Year's honours 2013) joined the bus at the Pimlico end and the bus's designer Thomas Heatherwick joined at Hampstead after its return, travelling on it as far as Tottenham Court Road on the second journey to Pimlico, which had Sir Peter at the wheel; Leon then resumed driving for the return trip to Hampstead Heath and the end of the first half of the duty.

LT32 picks up its passengers for the very first journey on Saturday morning, including one young boy who had reportedly been waiting for two hours so he could be first on the bus. Leon Daniels is driving. Despite being the day after the summer solstice and two days before midsummer, 22nd June was not a warm day so the cooling problems that were later to manifest did not become evident.

A factor with the LTs may be that the prototypes at Ash Grove were maintained by a member of Wright's staff who was in attendance four days a week, whereas at Holloway that garage's engineering staff took a greater role and the engineering specification was a big shift from what they had been used to with other buses at the garage. Daniels publicly praised the Metroline engineers for coping as they did. Problems reported in the first few days included electrical malfunctions, engine or battery overheating and power steering failures. In some buses, ceiling panels were coming away in service.

A big effort was made by all concerned to sort out why so many buses were breaking down – at least six were noted on the first Monday of operation – problems with the sophisticated electrics and power steering failures being among the main issues. Then, later in the month when the temperatures in London rose, it became apparent that the air-cooling system was not working effectively. Press references to the buses being 'saunas' or 'cauldrons' prompted another urgent investigation into what was happening. On the 38, the LTs also led to complaints about the inadequacy of the ventilation but the buses had been extras to the normal schedule, so on very hot days they could return to the garage. It is surprising however that the air-cooling problems had to reach such a high public profile before they were properly addressed. BBC London news reported in mid-September that consideration was being given to adding opening windows in the lower deck on future deliveries of the bus.

On the first Monday of operation, in common with a number of other LTs, LT24 has broken down. According to the driver, the power steering has failed. The rescue truck has arrived in Charing Cross Road to take it back to Holloway garage but first the recovery mechanic takes a look underneath.
For its tow, the bus will be lowered sufficiently to give adequate clearance at the back.
The buses delivered for the 24 also had some issues with the interiors, such as ceiling panels coming loose.

Assisting wheelchair passengers is an important part of the conductor's job. It is one that needs to be carried out sensitively as some of those in wheelchairs welcome the assistance while others insist on being independent. A shorter and two-door version of the bus, if retaining the rear door, would need to provide for wheelchairs to enter via the front entrance.

Holloway garage had an open day on Saturday 10th August and there was an opportunity to travel on an LT along the route taken by the buses to reach the 24 terminus at Hampstead Heath – via Tufnell Park, Kentish Town, Prince of Wales Road and then line of route to the terminus. Route number 639 was displayed in the windscreen and the bus used was LT24, which had taken part in the annual Imber event the previous Saturday. It still carried its special Imber route advertising, which it continued to do for some time after – much to the bemusement no doubt of any Londoners who noticed it.

Capital coverage 24/7 standard.co.uk

WEST END FINAL

London Evening Standard

ES

Kim Cattrall on vanity, menopause, money and men

PLUS

Back to the 1980s

FREE | READ BY 1.69 MILLION LONDONERS EVERY DAY

PLAY LIKE LION KINGS

COACH'S RALLYING CALL BEFORE THE CRUCIAL SERIES DECIDER

RUGBY SPECIAL PREVIEW: SPORT PAGES 80-84

PLUS MURRAY'S GIANT SEMI-FINAL TASK: PAGES 78-79

NEW ROUTEMASTERS HIT BY AIR-CON FAULTS

SWELTERING BORIS BUSES DUBBED THE 'CAULDRON ON WHEELS'

EXCLUSIVE

... AND THE HEAT'S ON ANDY MURRAY TOO

Following an *Evening Standard* front page headline about the 'Sweltering Boris Buses' on Friday 5th July, a weekend of intensive attempts to solve the problem took place. The following Wednesday, the *Standard* reported that 'London's transport commissioner today vowed that problems with soaring temperatures on the new Boris bus had been solved'. It went on to report that 'Sir Peter Hendy and designer Thomas Heatherwick were spotted last night with thermometers testing the heat in an empty bus as it circled Kings Cross', the workplace and home of Heatherwick. Leon Daniels tells us that he also was on the bus and that it was at 2pm the trip was made rather than in the evening, but perhaps they were lucky in the choice of bus as the problem had not in fact been solved. The following week a company that had not previously been involved with the bus, Birmingham-based Grayson Thermal Systems, was appointed by Wrightbus to get things sorted. A programme was quickly drawn up, the work on each bus taking the best part of a week.

Wrightbus made progressive improvements in the weight of the LTs during the latter half 2013. The LTs on route 24 (LTs 9-40) were 12460kg and could legally carry 80. Those delivered for the 11 (LTs 41-68) were labelled as 12320kg and had a legal limit of 82 passengers and those delivered for route 9 (LTs 69-94) were 12200kg and could carry 84 legally. LTs 95-117, for route 390, were slightly heavier at 12220kg but had the same legal load as LTs 69-94. Fluctuations in weight were to continue. In the calculation of the maximum load the conductor is not counted, so the capacity is the same whether or not there is one on board.

The heating and cooling system on the LTs was specified in the contract to keep the inside temperature between 15 and 21 degrees, but temperatures above 30 degrees were recorded. On one of the hot summer days of 2013 a Routemaster overtakes LT18 to give a comparison of rear ends and a good impression of the new bus's highly reflective exterior.

Route 11 was selected as the second route to be fully converted to LT operation and was scheduled for phased conversion from Saturday 21st September. Conductors were trained, like those with Metroline, in four groups which each spent ten days on the road and five days in the classroom. Training began on 2nd September and the last new conductors completed their training on the Tuesday following the first buses starting on the 11, but by the time the first one entered service on the evening of Friday 20th September the target for completion of the changeover had slipped from Wednesday 25th to the middle of the following week; it subsequently slipped further. The first day the morning run-out on the 11 was 100% LTs was 15th October. The period of over three weeks taken for this conversion suggests the buses may have been undergoing engineering attention.

The conductors on the 11 were each equipped with iPads. With these, they can sign on to begin their duties at Fulham Broadway, the Victoria Coach Station eastbound or westbound stops or Liverpool Street (all 24 conductors sign on at the Hampstead Heath terminus, where there is a facility in the staff hut there). The iPads also contain details of their duty rota, travel enquiry information and a form for reporting any incidents. In 2014 tablet computers or iPads were issued to conductors at Stamford Brook, Clapton and Holloway also. As with Metroline, applications from people with experience in customer service and retail work made up a good proportion of those who were recruited.

On the first weekend of LTs on route 11, LT42 is followed by WVL130 in Whitehall. A phased changeover had been planned, but the timescale was greater than had been intended. Surface Transport MD Leon Daniels drove LT59 on route 11 the day before its conversion began, leaving Liverpool Street for Victoria at 6.21pm. He did similar pre-conversion trips on routes 9, 390 and 453. The Stockwell blinds also included the N11 and 88.

Not only are the customer assistants not able to take fares, they are trained not to get into arguments with anyone who refuses to touch in their Oyster card or show a pass. One passenger I saw doing just this got the response: 'If revenue gets on mate, it's your fine not mine'. In the first few days of the 11, revenue inspectors were more in evidence than they had been in the first few days of the 24, suggesting some degree of fare loss was being suffered on conversion to LT. The presence of a second member of staff does however make it more likely that someone will pay their fare than running a bus with three possible points of entry with driver only. CAs were instructed to take a slightly more proactive role in revenue protection during 2014. The conductors are a very popular feature, dealing with a variety of situations in a friendly and efficient way. In the first three months of the 24 there had been no formal compensation claims involving conductors, though there had been a few cases of minor platform accidents. It was only a matter of time before a serious incident and on 4th October a woman fell off a 24 and sustained a head injury that was initially life threatening.

A few days before the 11 started, customer assistants at Holloway garage began to receive the first elements of their uniform. They were also given name badges in a modern incarnation of the 20th century PSV badges which showed the conductor's number. Then, route 11 conductors started to receive badges soon after they began work and later conversions followed suit.

The recruits for the 24 were told that 9,000 people had approached the company to apply for the job, including 800-900 from one advert in the *Metro* newspaper alone. The 11 attracted 2,500 enquiries before applications closed on 19th July. Of these, 250 were selected from their CVs, whittled down through a process of group interview and one to one interview to select the 57 conductors needed. Two of the best ambassadors for London buses are seen here. Route 11's conductors, one of whom checks his computer, were trained to stand by the door, as seen in the second view, but by November they had mostly moved to the conventional position as on other routes.

LT62 in Chelsea Bridge Road on 22nd September 2013, having collided with a car and run into the back of a single-deck bus.

On its second day in service, at around 1pm on Sunday 22nd September, LT62 was involved in a serious accident while operating on route 11. As the bus approached the traffic lights at the junction of Lower Sloane Street and Pimlico Road, the driver is reported to have had a problem with the brakes. The bus continued 'at speed' past the red traffic lights and along Chelsea Bridge Road until colliding with a car and crashing into the back of a single-deck bus on route 360. The driver of the LT and the two occupants of the car were taken to hospital with serious injuries and it is very fortunate that no-one was killed. The conductor (who acted commendably and calmly to warn those on board to prepare for an impact) and 12 passengers suffered bruising but no major harm. An immediate investigation was set up and a team of engineers urgently sent to check out the other LTs at Stockwell garage. The conductor of the crashed bus, who had suffered a bruised back, was at work again on the Tuesday, accompanied by another fully trained customer assistant to enable her to rest as needed. As the new buses were falling behind in being available for service over half of the trained conductors had no work to do immediately but were of course paid.

In the eighteen months following the introduction of LTs on route 24, nine of the type (LTs 35, 62, 96, 100, 106, 124, 128, 175, 262) crashed into something or other buses including three other LTs (22, 138, 161). Two further such incidents occurred on two consecutive days in February 2015 during the conversion of route 55, when LT360 was badly damaged inside Hackney garage on the 3rd and LT315 ran into the back of DW516 on the 4th. One accident involving a stationary bus at traffic lights occurred when a speeding car ran into LT176 whilst it was working on the N38 early on the morning of 4th June 2014. All the occupants of the car were killed and the LT suffered substantial damage.

Opposite: Heatherwick was keen to avoid the posting of a plethora of notices, but the bus needs to display all those on other London double deckers plus a few more.

This staircase
leads to an
open platform

Watch out for
moving traffic

For your safety
Please do not stand on the upper deck or stairs
£80 penalty fare or
prosecution
CCTV cameras
in operation
No smoking

Emergency
Exit
In case of
emergency push
in white areas and
pull to remove panel

Emergency
door
release
Push here

Emergency
door
control

Buggy users please make space for wheelchair users
Priority
wheelchair area
Baby buggies

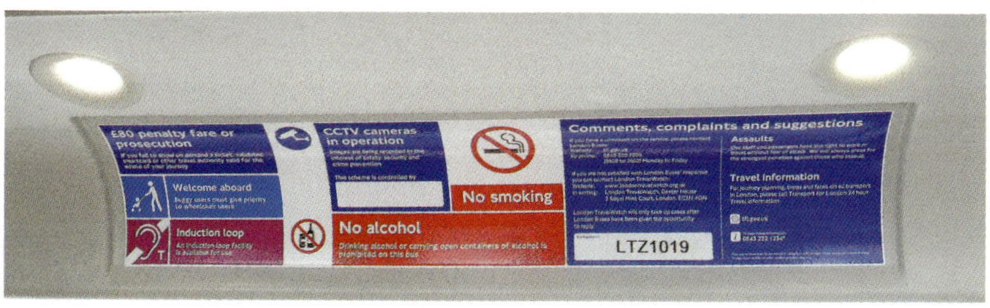
£80 penalty fare or
prosecution
CCTV cameras
in operation
No smoking
Comments, complaints and suggestions
Welcome aboard
Induction loop
No alcohol
LTZ1019

Priority seats
for people who are disabled,
pregnant or less able to stand

Cyclists
Stay back

oyster
Contactless payments
accepted:
On boarding
please touch
your card flat
on the reader
Cash users
must pay
driver

oyster
Contactless payments
accepted:
Please touch
your card flat
on the reader

Passengers must
not stand beyond
this point
Please do not speak to or obscure
the driver's vision while the bus
is moving

SETTLING DOWN

JAMES WHITING

The conversion following route 11, that of route 9, was carried out in one go on Saturday 26th October 2013. It was operated with conductors on Mondays to Fridays only. The same applied to the next route, the 390, in December, when route 24 changed from daily operation with conductors to Monday to Friday only. Then it became known that the first conversion of 2014, route 148, would be one-person operated at all times. Another development was a trial reinstatement of conductors on route 38 from 4th November. The trial, on Mondays to Fridays, involved switching from two-person operation to opo, or vice versa, during the journey, the switchover point being Mildmay Park. Four Ash Grove drivers were persuaded to volunteer to be conductors on the basis that it was for four weeks only. The times of the duties, all of which started and finished at Mildmay Park, were: 1014-1205 and 1545-1939; 0836-1331 and 1724-1915; 0719-1120 and 1225-1642; 0705-1055 and 1205-1615, giving two morning peak hour journeys serving central London with conductors and two evening peak hour trips. The operation of shutting and locking the rear doors can be done in less than a minute, as can the unlocking and opening in the reverse direction. The trial opened up the possibility of having conductors on parts of routes only, a sensible development that would make the best use of the second on-board staff member. The existence of the rear door also meant that if a conductor was delayed getting to his or her bus, the bus could continue in service in opo mode. The four-week trial turned out, as expected, to be a prelude to the full conversion of route 38 to LT operation using conductors in 2014. Towards the end of 2013, Arriva advertised for applications from would-be customer assistants.

By the time of route 9's conversion, the buses were running more reliably, with fewer breakdowns being noted. LT71 makes the turn from Pall Mall into St James's Street. Most exterior advertising on the newly converted 9 route was for the The Book of Mormon, continuing a tendency for most such advertising in the early days to be for London musicals. Route 9 being one of the two heritage routes, the hop on, hop off facility was provided by RMs seven days a week for most of its length until the Routemasters were withdrawn on 26th July 2014.

LT93 alongside a poster announcing the route's conversion to the type. The same design of poster was used for routes 24, 11 and 390. When in opo mode the rear door has the curved section remain shut to avoid the risk of a boarding passenger getting hit in the face by its closing. The front door remains the most used as seen in the lower view at Green Park station. LTs on the route at first carried black on yellow running number plates but these were changed at TfL's request to yellow on black, so that the plates blended in with the black panel on which they are displayed. Yellow on black or white on black plates have become the norm for this type.

As recorded earlier in this book, LT100 was on loan to Ipswich Transport between 25th and 29th November, the first use of an LT by an operator outside London. Ipswich used the bus on its town centre shuttle service, coincidentally numbered 38. Ipswich Buses' Managing Director said just before its arrival: 'We're confident that the Borismaster is going to make quite a stir on the streets of Ipswich and we're thrilled at the prospect of getting people thinking, talking and even tweeting about buses'. In the event it failed to make much of an impression on the people of Ipswich.

The continuing use of the name Borismaster here and elsewhere was something that TfL were keen to counter. The following week, the press release for route 390's conversion spoke of the buses (for the first time in an official announcement) as New Routemasters. TfL also sent out three separate tweets about the conversion, all using the words New Routemasters. The bus stop publicity panels along the route of the 390, posted shortly before the visit to Ipswich, made no mention of an official name for the bus, so it was a swift decision. The names Borismaster and Boris Bus persisted outside TfL alongside references to New Routemaster and were at least rather more original. Many names had been suggested for the New Bus for London by people outside TfL and at one point it was proposed to have a public competition to find the best one, but this idea was not pursued. Leon Daniels's favourite among the unsolicited names suggested was Retromaster. Most of the new LTs delivered to Arriva for route 38's full conversion to the type received rear staircase plates showing the new name in place of the New Bus for London plates fitted to earlier buses.

Route 390 was converted to LT operation on 7th December with conductors on Mondays to Fridays only, Metroline's Holloway garage thereby becoming the first to operate two LT routes. From day one, the buses for the 24 and 390 were mixed and it was not long before crews were mixed also. The 390 conversion went smoothly and brought passenger service with the new bus to Oxford Street for the first time.

Right: 2013 drew to a close with four routes operated by the New Bus for London: 9, 11, 24 and 390. Of these, the 390 was the route that had most recently had a full allocation of Routemasters, which it had lost in September 2004. Route 11 was now the only one to have conductors at weekends. LT28 is seen under the Oxford Street Christmas illuminations.

The plates on the rear interior wall of the LT changed name during the new deliveries for the 38. Chassis plates continue to show 'NBFL'.

Archway
390
LTZ 1028
VLA144

Not all buses are pleasing to the eye after dark, though any bus looks good if it is a cold or wet night and you have been waiting for its arrival. Heatherwick's bus has clearly been designed to look good in all conditions, not least because its internal lighting does not bombard the senses in the way that fluorescent tubes do. The softer glow of the interior emphasises the shape of the staircase glazing and the spotlights have the appearance of a cosy but modern kitchen in a smart London apartment. It does not look out of place in the most expensive parts of the city.

LT67 in Sloane Square and LT3 in Piccadilly.

Overleaf: LT59 at St Paul's, LT29 in Victoria Street, LT8 in Shaftesbury Avenue, LT85 at the Royal Albert Hall.

Liverpool Street 11
Go Ahead London
LT59
Discover London's best events
KweekWeek
Event discovery & ticketing
11 Liverpool Street
LTZ 1059

LandSecurities
Pimlico 24
149
SB
HOUSE OF FRASER
LTZ 1029

Victoria 38
LT12 HHT

KweekWeek
Discover London's best events
Download our FREE app
LONDON UNITED
LT85

Below: LT2 in Theatreland and LT37 in Oxford Street.

Opposite top: Posters announcing the 2014 fares increases included computer generated images of the different modes and to represent buses an illustration based on the NBfL mock-up MN0123 was used.

Opposite margin: Advert in the London *Metro* in December for customer assistants for the 38.

Opposite bottom left: Two Lambert Souvenirs postcards show New Routemasters at Trafalgar Square.

Opposite bottom right: The first bus stop publicity for the name New Routemaster.

Prior to the last conversion of 2013, it had been announced on 5th December that route 148 would be converted to LT on 15th February 2013. The big departure on this conversion was that the buses would be operated with a driver only at all times. Statements along the lines that it had always been the intention that only some of the 600 buses ordered would have conductors may well be true from TfL's point of view but it was not in line with what had originally been pledged by Boris.

TfL's wish for the New Bus for London to appear on picture postcards was realised at the start of 2014 when Lambert Souvenirs issued two different views, one showing an LT and an RM side by side opposite its shop and registered office at the northern end of Whitehall and another showing two LTs, a front and a rear, plus a London taxi at the same spot. RMs remained very much in the majority on London postcards though, as they did in the plethora of souvenirs that featured London buses. In January it was announced that the heritage RMs on route 9, that had been running alongside open platform LTs since October 2013 would be withdrawn in July 2014. The route had the anomaly while the two types shared it of having conductors on the RMs circulating to collect fares and check tickets whilst the LT customer assistants remained on the platform. On two-manned LTs in general, during the period – up to 5th July 2014 – when cash fares were still being taken on London buses, the small minority of passengers who wanted to pay this way were directed, usually to their surprise, by the conductor to the driver.

In January 2014 came the first LT in a livery other than the standard red. On the 27th of the month, LT150 in a basically silver livery was used to launch TfL's Year of the Bus outside City Hall, where LT1 had appeared in December 2011. Part painted and part vinyled, the bus entered service on route 9 on 5th February, the first day of a two-day tube strike, which also saw a number of LTs enter service early on the 148. Other liveries that had been proposed for LTs in the Year of the Bus were LGOC, red with cream band, Shillibeer and all-over LT seat moquette pattern. The idea of using an LGOC scheme was revived later in the year when LT60 received General livery. LT150 was already red when chosen to be the first silver one so was sprayed silver with the red masked to make the bands. Originally the silver would have been relieved with one red horizontal stripe but Heatherwick came up with lines that follow the bus contours. Leon Daniels tells us that 'the specification of the width of the striping was urgently needed but in the rush misquoted to Wrights so, as outshopped, looked awful – rather like thick red lipstick. There was no time to redo it so silver tape was run along the red striping and finished just before the launch'.

The full conversion of the 148 went ahead as planned on 15th February. It is rather ironic that the first route to have been publicised from the start as being converted to 'New Routemasters' should be the first to operate them with a driver only. This confused some, including the London SE1 community website, which looked forward to 'the return of open platform buses' – describing them as 'the first such vehicles to operate over Westminster Bridge since the withdrawal of Routemasters from the 159 in December 2005'.

LT122 does the honours under a dramatic sky for this classic London view of Westminster Bridge and Parliament. Without conductors, the point of having three doors on the bus is somewhat reduced. They may sometimes shorten times at bus stops but scheduled running times are not changed, nor are any buses saved. Apart from the completion of route 38, only the 10 was converted to LTs with conductors in 2014. Many CAs were not expecting their job to last beyond 2016.

Above: LT150 at the western end of Piccadilly after the Year of the Bus launch on 27th January 2014.

Left: The front and nearside of the bus are shown as it passes Aldwych in service from Stamford Brook garage. It initially worked on route 9 and then on route 10 when it was converted in April. It has special advertising with the words: 'You're looking at one of the most technologically advanced buses in the world'. It also carries the Year of the Bus logo on the side in common with a number of other buses during 2014.

This broadside offside view shows the skilful addition of silver coloured tape to amend the deep red stripes the bus had been delivered with. The Year of the Bus was placed in the hands of Exterion Media to promote and their logo appears alongside the special roundel. The smaller photos show a close up view of the silver tape and the fleetnames of other companies who ran the silver painted buses. The two with Arriva did not carry fleetnames.

d
We'll have 600 of these ultramodern buses in operation by 2016
TRANSPORT FOR LONDON
LONDON UNITED
RATP GROUP
LT150
YEAR OF THE BUS 2014
ExterionMedia
WORKING TOGETHER TO CELEBRATE YEAR OF THE BUS

Metroline
A member of
ComfortDelGro
LT190
24

Stagecoach
Bow

Among the official Year of the Bus souvenirs were a key ring and a fridge magnet. They were included in 'Evolution of the London Bus' sets showing progress in bus design over 100 years.

An A6 size guide was issued to New Routemaster drivers and customer assistants in January 2014 detailing the responsibilities of each role. Within London Buses, the vehicles are referred to as NRMs. The cover of the guide is shown here actual size and some pages from it are reproduced by kind permission of TfL on the next three pages.

Foreword

Back in February 2012, I launched the first of eight New Routemaster (NRM) prototype vehicles on Route 38. Just over a year later, the first full route (24) converted to these stunning vehicles.

The NRM not only oozes style but is a testament to British design, engineering and, above all, innovation. As well as delivering significant environmental benefits, it also reinstates the traditional hop-on, hop-off rear platform.

By ordering large numbers of these fantastic machines we are also creating UK jobs. I promised to expand the NRM fleet and I am confident they will be as iconic in London as red phone boxes, Big Ben and Beefeaters.

You should be immensely proud to work on these unique buses, and I am sure you will do your best to provide London's bus users with the world class service for which we are rightly accredited.

Thank you.

Boris Johnson
Mayor of London

Introduction to the NRM

The NRM is the first bus to be designed for the Capital's streets in more than 50 years.

As a driver or customer assistant working on these unique vehicles, you are an ambassador for London's bus service and have a great opportunity to show the world what a truly first class customer experience we can provide.

This guide summarises the key features and operating procedures of the bus and explains how customers will use it. It also outlines your particular responsibilities, either as a driver or customer assistant.

Further guidance

The information contained in this guide supplements the third (2012) edition of the Big Red Book. It generally applies when the bus is operating in crew mode with both a driver and customer assistant.

If you are a driver working on your own and driving the bus in one-person operation (OPO) mode, you should also refer to the relevant guidance in the Big Red Book.

Operating the NRM

Normal operation in crew mode

1) When the driver presses the 'Door Open' button, both the front and middle door will open at once.

2) After closing the doors, the driver's information screen shows a 'red man'. This means the door/brake interlock is on

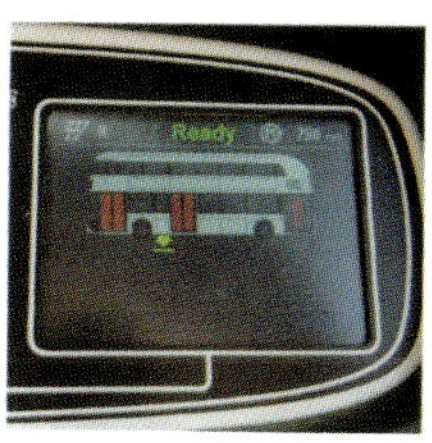

3) The customer assistant should first check for any passengers still intending to board, then release the door/brake interlock by pressing and holding the green interlock release button until it stops beeping - generally about five seconds

4) A 'green man' on the driver's information screen will indicate that the door/brake interlock is off and the bus is ready to proceed

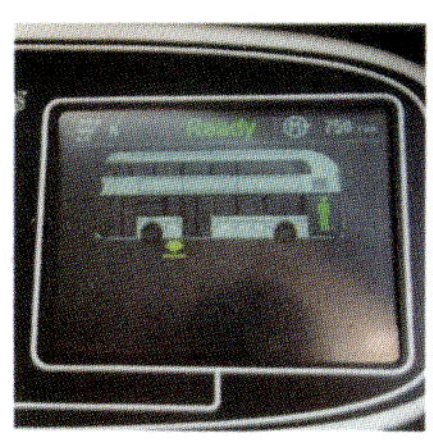

5) Drivers should check for boarding/alighting using the mirrors and/or CCTV until they are satisfied they can set off safely

6) Customer assistants can let the driver know of any potential problems, such as a passenger attempting to board/alight, by repeatedly pressing their orange alert button (also located in the inset area by the rear staircase). If the bus has already pulled away, the driver should stop the vehicle as soon as it is safe to do so, discuss the problem with the customer assistant and seek help, perhaps by contacting CentreComm

Additional guidance for customer assistants

Your uniform

All customer assistants will be given the same uniform, irrespective of your operating company. This is to give NRM buses a unifying look and feel.

You will also be supplied with a special name badge. Please wear it with pride at all times while you are on duty.

The badge will look like this:

Using a hand-held device

If your company has issued you with a hand-held device, such as a tablet PC, use it in accordance with their instructions when answering passengers' questions.

Overhead (emergency) door buttons

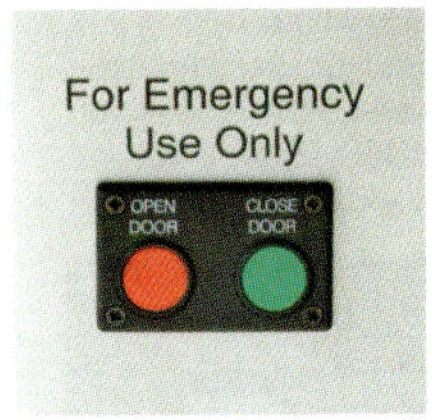

Converting the bus from crew to OPO mode

1) The driver should check the handbrake is on and the engine is running

2) The driver then presses the yellow crew button in the cab and an icon will appear on their information screen

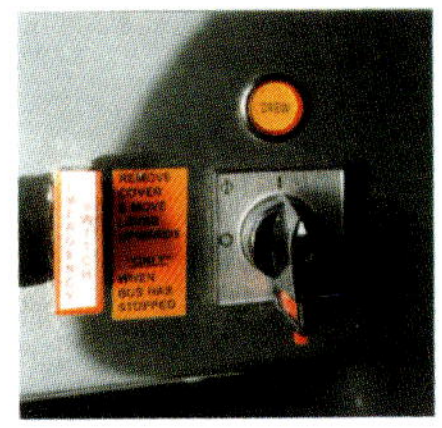

3) The customer assistant should press and hold their orange lock button (located in the inset area by the rear staircase) until they can hear the air pressure release. An alarm will then sound

Additional guidance for customer assistants

Converting the bus from crew to OPO mode

4) The customer assistant then moves the curved, quarter-panel door into the correct closed/nested position, keeping hands and fingers clear of the hand pole

5) The customer assistant should press and hold the orange lock button again until they hear the air pressure being released

6) The final step is for the customer assistant to close the three-quarter rear door using the overhead green emergency button

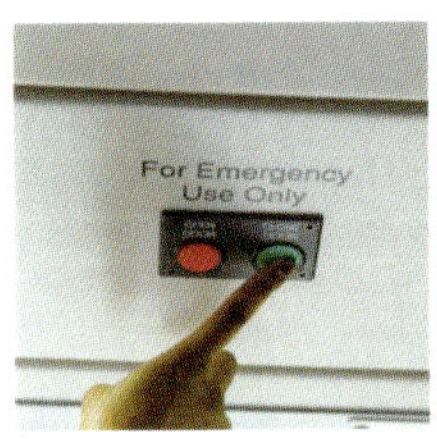

7) Pressing the green interlock release button will stop the alarm

Converting the bus from OPO to crew mode

1) Check the handbrake is on and the engine is running

2) The customer assistant opens the three-quarter rear door using the overhead red emergency button

Additional guidance for customer assistants

Converting the bus from OPO to crew mode

3) The driver then presses the yellow crew button inside the cab. An icon will appear on their information screen

4) The customer assistant should press and hold the orange lock button until they hear the air pressure release and an alarm sound

5) The customer assistant moves the curved quarter-panel door into an open position, taking care that it does not foul the overhead coving panel

6) They should then press and hold the orange lock button again until they can hear the air pressure being released

7) The alarm can be stopped by pressing the green interlock release button

8) Finally, the customer assistant confirms with the driver that the crew light in the cab has been switched off. The driver may need to do this by pressing the yellow crew button

Key points to remember

- The NRM can be operated in either OPO mode, with just a driver, or crew mode, with both a driver and customer assistant. The rear platform (and door) is open in crew mode. The driver operates all three doors, including the rear door, when the bus is in OPO mode
- The driver is responsible for passenger safety and comfort at all times, whether a customer assistant is on board or not, and for checking the bus when it is on a stand. Check the bus regularly for unattended bags or packages, with the customer assistant's help when available
- The customer assistant should normally stand at the rear open platform to help people on and off safely, both at stops and between stops. They should patrol the bus to check for unusual or suspicious activity, including unattended items

- Customer assistants must not collect fares or validate Oyster cards, but can direct passengers to card readers (available at all three doors) or those wishing to pay by cash to the driver
- Drivers are responsible for informing passengers about any change of destination or unscheduled stops due to breakdown, and for issuing transfer vouchers to all customers. Both the driver and customer assistant should help people transfer to other buses, and check transfer vouchers presented by anyone transferring from another bus
- The NRM is designed to help older and disabled passengers travel safely and comfortably. All buses can kneel to make getting on and off easier and have a step-free gangway on the lower deck, a wheelchair ramp, dedicated space for wheelchair users and a T-loop system transmitting announcements for those using hearing aids
- Both the driver and customer assistant should be ready to offer help if a passenger is having difficulty and should give wheelchair users priority. However, if other passengers insist on occupying the wheelchair space, even after you have requested they move to make room for a wheelchair user, you cannot ask them to leave the bus
- When the bus is in crew mode, passengers should never be prevented from using the open rear platform to board or alight between stops, although the customer assistant should advise if it is not safe to do so. Driving close to the kerb in heavy traffic will reduce the risk to passengers hopping on or off

Route 148's Scania double deckers, together with those on route 10 which followed with LTs on 26th April, were partly re-employed to replace Tridents on route 281 and partly, after refurbishment, used on route E3 from 31st May when London United took over that route from Metroline. Only one of the first eight routes converted to LT was converted at the time of its contract renewal, this being the 8/N8. The additional cascading of vehicles was something that had to be taken into account therefore. The first main LT route, the 24, had recently had some new Volvo B5LH hybrids introduced to it in and these moved to route 52. The 24's Volvo B9TLs were moved to Alperton where they were used to convert route 245 to double-deck operation. The Volvo B7TLs on routes 9 and 11 were nine and ten years old respectively and so the time was about right for them to move on. The B7TLs of similar vintage on the 390 at Holloway stayed at the garage and allowed five-year old Enviro400s to replace older Tridents at Potters Bar. On route 38, a large number of Wrightbus Gemini 2s new in 2009/10 were displaced, mostly being used to replace all remaining Euro II DAFs, most of which were 14 years old, at Croydon and Brixton garages.

The net effect was to increase the number of low-emission buses in service, particularly in central London. Emissions have been one of the main selling points of the NBfL, with the Millbrook test results frequently quoted by TfL until in-service figures were issued in October 2014 claiming increased mpg of between 38% and 57% compared with buses previously operated, representing fuel savings of between 27.5% and 36% on the buses surveyed (not as was inferred in some quarters as fuel savings of 'over half'). Real service conditions can never match the simulated service conditions of a test environment but there were concerns when the production vehicles entered service about fuel consumption, and therefore emissions, being quite a lot higher than anticipated. It was certainly noticeable when travelling on LTs in 2013 and 2014 that some buses were running the engine for much longer periods than others.

Increasingly demanding emissions regulations rendered the Euro V specification of the buses out of date and by spring of 2014 a few buses to Euro VI standards were delivered. LT8, which had returned to Wrightbus in October 2013, was the first prototype conversion to be done. Euro VI legislation focuses on exhaust after-treatment systems that reduce nitrogen oxide (NOx) emissions to a very small level, with reductions of up to 95% being claimed. First, the exhaust gases from the engine are internally recirculated and the engine runs hotter to burn them up. Second, a system known as selective catalytic reduction uses a urea/water solution injected into the exhaust system to treat the remaining NOx raw emissions and reduce carbon dioxide emissions also. Euro V engines needed one of these two systems; Euro VI engines need both.

The Euro VI changes added 240kg to the weight of LT8, bringing its legal passenger capacity down to 74 and making this bus the heaviest ever to have been operated on a regular London bus route. Industry figures quoted variations of additional weight for Euro VI engines of up to 185kg. However, not only did LT8 go beyond this, a new ADL Enviro with a Euro VI engine delivered to Stagecoach in May was 270kg heavier than its Euro V predecessors. The Euro VI New Routemasters of the first production batch (273-311) weighed 12430kg, giving a capacity of 81 passengers.

High Street Kensington, where LT161 is seen, and Oxford Street each gained a second LT route with the conversion of route 10. The LTs from Stamford Brook and Shepherd's Bush garages were fitted with common blinds for routes 9, 10 and 148.

LT8 had returned to Wrightbus in October 2013 and re-entered service, allocated to Metroline's Holloway garage, with Euro VI specification in July 2014. This bus and the later batch of LTs allocated to Holloway had the Comfort DelGro names in all-white to conform to the design standards laid down by TfL for the LTs.

Following the conversions of routes 148 and 10, it was the turn of the 38 to receive new LTs to join the four prototypes still at work on it. This batch of LTs displayed a weight of 12140kgs, making them the lightest so far if correct. The first four of the new buses to run on the 38 entered service on 29th April, the first of a pair of consecutive tube strike days. By 21st June a full allocation could be provided on the 38 and N38 and, two days earlier, the first LTs entered service on the 8 and N8. The rest followed fairly quickly so that by the second week of July only two of Bow's allocation were still to appear.

LT196 passes the old Hackney Public Baths with LT216 travelling in the opposite direction. LTs for the 38 entered service before the fitting of exterior advert frames, as had the new buses delivered for route 10's conversion, and very smart they looked.

Conversions of 24-hour routes 10, 24, 148 and 390 included the LTs on both day and night elements. With the 9 and 11 the long extensions of routes N9 and N11, compared with the daytime routes, led to a decision not to use LTs on these, though route number N11 was included on Stockwell's LT blinds. The first N prefixed route to use LTs was the N38 (Victoria to Walthamstow Central), a conversion that saw the LTs first operating in service beyond Zone 2. Route N8 was also allocated LTs, taking the type to Hainault, a terminus within a few yards of the Essex county border.

LT257 stands at the temporary central London terminus of routes 8 and N8, owing to Crossrail works, in August 2014. It was the second N prefixed night route to receive the buses. The first LT on an N prefixed route had been LT178 on the N38 on Friday 16th May. In addition to 8 and N8, Bow's LTs had the 15, N15 and 205X on their blinds. Clapton's had 73 and N73 in readiness for their conversion.

On 22nd June 2014, the first anniversary of the entry into service of LTs on the 24, TfL held a very successful Year of the Bus parade in Regent Street with bus designs on display spanning over 100 years, the oldest being parked at the Piccadilly Circus end. It was a hot, sunny day and the parade attracted a large number of people. Three LTs were parked at the top of Regent Street, LTs 6, 239 and 150.

The first Euro VI Boris Buses to enter service were LTs 172 and 188, which started work from Clapton garage on route 38 on 4th July 2014, joined the day after by LT 173 and on the 7th by prototype LT8. The Euro VI LTs are known not to have settled in well initially, with battery and electrical problems again featuring. LTs 172 and 173, for example were out of service for a good part of July. The first three Euro VI LTs were followed by LT189 with London General at Stockwell and LT190 with Metroline at Holloway. Apart from LT173, the Euro VI prototypes from the production batch were painted silver. Silver livery was also carried by LTs 150, mentioned earlier, and 256, 271 and 272. The silver livery was joined by bus garage open days and a parade of buses in Regent Street on 22nd June as further elements of TfL's Year of the Bus, as was the dressing of 32 LTs in all-over adverts for Adidas as detailed in the chapter after next. There was also a Bus Sculpture Trail involving one metre high sculptures of New Routemasters displayed in streets, parks and public spaces. In common with a separate trail of fifty Paddington Bear statues at about the same time, the bus statues were to be sold off for charity at the end of the display period.

Arriva's LT172 at Piccadilly Circus shows the red banding as applied to the silver LTs that followed LT150.

With the conversion of route 8 to LT, at a time when the route was curtailed at Tottenham Court Road owing to Crossrail construction works, Bloomsbury Street became the first thoroughfare to have four LT routes run along it, the first to have three being Victoria Street upon route 148's conversion. The wider spaced characters on the registration plate of LT16 are typical of the re-registered buses.

In the summer of 2014 there were new reports of cooling system problems, but it seems likely that these resulted from isolated journeys on a few buses where the system was not working properly. Having travelled on quite a number of LTs on hot summer days in 2014, I found very few problems upstairs except in the front seats, where the cooling system is ineffective. The lower deck is not pleasant to travel in on such days, but then few buses are. Direct comparisons downstairs between the LTs, a Wright/Gemini and even an RM revealed little difference in temperature. There were people fanning themselves on the Gemini just as there were on the LTs. The LTs running in opo mode were however generally found to be a little warmer than those whose open platforms allowed some of the heat from the engine to escape.

Numbers of complaints received about temperatures in the LTs were an area where TfL refused to answer Freedom of Information requests and it does seem at least possible that some of the complaints were from people who were politically opposed to the bus. A TfL statement on the issue said: 'The air cooling system on New Routemasters is now working effectively on virtually all vehicles in the fleet as verified by assurance checks carried out early in the summer'. TfL also stated that it did not advocate more powerful air cooling systems on buses as it was striking a balance between comfort and minimising fuel consumption, the cooling system being powered by the batteries and so ultimately the diesel engine.

‘Mollycoddling conductors must stop lecturing on Boris bus safety’

Martin Bentham
Home Affairs Editor

Open platform: the new Routemaster

A HOME Office minister has called on Boris Johnson to tell “mollycoddling” conductors to “back off” and stop lecturing passengers about safety on London’s new Routemaster buses.

Norman Baker said he was fed up with being told by conductors not to stand on the open platform at the rear as he waited to get off.

The Lib-Dem MP also criticised conductors for attempting to block passengers who want to jump on as buses move off and insisted that it was time for the Mayor to “take away the cotton wool” that was spoiling enjoyment of the buses.

His criticism echoes similar complaints from other passengers that the value of the Routemasters’ open platform is being undermined by an overly cautious approach to safety.

Transport for London promised to remind bus operators that passengers should be allowed to use the platform when preparing to get off, but insisted that safety remained its priority.

It admitted, however, that its statistics showed that only one passenger is hurt boarding or alighting for every million journeys made on the Routemasters.

Mr Baker said the figures confirmed that the risk of any accident was overblown and insisted that the public should be allowed to stand on the open platform without being subjected to hectoring comments from the conductor.

He added: “It is right to have reintroduced platform buses, but why are we being mollycoddled? When people want to get on and off they should be able to do it without being told by the conductors that it’s not safe to stand there on the open platform.

“My message to Boris is take away the cotton wool and let the buses be used as they were intended. He should tell his conductors to back off.”

Mr Baker, a former transport minister, said he believed that interference by conductors was sometimes putting passengers at greater, not lesser, risk.

He added: “The other day I ran for the bus and tried to jump on as it moved off and had a conductor trying to block my way, which was far more dangerous. I still got on though.”

The “Boris bus” was introduced in February 2012 following an election pledge by the Mayor to commission a modern version of London’s traditional Routemaster, which allowed passengers to get on and off between stops via its open platform.

Mike Weston, TfL’s director of buses, said: “We are working closely with the operators of new Routemasters to ensure that training for conductors allows them to balance the benefits of an open platform with the need for safety.”

In the London *Evening Standard* of 18th June 2014 comments by Home Office minister Norman Baker highlighted the over-caution frequently exercised by Boris Bus conductors with people wanting to board or alight between stops. It was very common for people to be told not to step off a stationary bus even when up against the pavement and to many conductors the rear platform was a no-go area for passengers except at bus stops. This over-caution was stated by TfL as something it was in touch with the operators about so that the right balance between the benefits of an open platform and safety could be achieved.

BEYOND LONDON

KEITH MCGILLIVRAY

Whether they realise it or not, Londoners have benefited from consistent investment in new buses for years. Between them, the many bus operators in London have historically received hundreds of new buses on an annual basis, with regular platoons of Wright Geminis, ADL Enviros and many other vehicle types arriving on an almost ongoing basis. Perhaps it took Boris Johnson's bold spirit and such a highly specific design brief to develop a bus that turned heads and engendered a sense of ownership amongst London's travelling public of "their" new bus. When Boris Johnson first announced his vision of a New Bus for London, he did so in response to a highly charged political backdrop about the safety and suitability of articulated buses in the capital. This being the case, it seems very unlikely that he considered the transferability of such a specific design to provincial UK bus operations and beyond.

Ipswich Buses was the first non-London operator (excluding the Imber events) to have operated one in passenger service. Despite recent orders of new ADL Enviro 200s, it has been some years since the fleet ordered brand-new double deck buses; indeed, not long before, the company purchased mid-life low-floor buses from London. The story of how a New Routemaster came to operate on the streets of Ipswich begins in April 2013, when Suffolk County Council issued a tender for the operation of the Ipswich Park and Ride contract from November 2013 onwards. Ipswich Buses had operated park and ride services in the town from 1997 until 2008, when First Eastern Counties was awarded the five-year contract. Following a new tender award, the successful bidder would commence operations in early November 2013.

At the time the tender was issued, Ipswich Buses' Managing Director, Malcolm Robson was President of the Confederation for Passenger Transport. During his tenure as CPT President, Malcolm met with Peter Hendy, Transport for London's Commissioner, and raised the question of whether Ipswich Buses might be permitted a trial of a New Routemaster. Malcolm's intention was to run the New Routemaster in and around the park and ride sites during April 2013, allowing rival bidders to form the view that the Ipswich Buses submission would propose the use of such vehicles. Although an agreement for the trial was made in principle, a bus could not be made available until May 2013, and in that instance LT5 visited the town as part of an event at Ipswich Transport Museum and did not operate in service.

In November 2013, by which time Ipswich Buses had been awarded the park and ride contract, LT100 visited the town for a week-long loan. It was to be used on service 38, the Ipswich town centre shuttle which is sponsored by Suffolk County Council. The terms of the loan were that the New Routemaster was only to be operated by drivers who had received training on the vehicle from TfL instructors and that no ticket machine or cash vault was to be fitted. Both of TfL's

LT100 during its week-long use in Ipswich on park and ride work.

conditions were easily satisfied by placing the bus into use on service 38 which takes approximately fifteen minutes end to end, and is free to all users. For the duration of its stay in Ipswich, LT100 operated in diesel mode only. During the trial, LT100 attracted significant attention from local news media, including the Ipswich Star and Radio Suffolk, which carried out a Vox Pop survey of those who travelled on the vehicle.

Malcolm Robson indicated that he was disappointed with the general feedback offered by passengers during the Vox Pop; many users revealed that they thought it was no better or worse than vehicles that typically operate the service. Malcolm recalled his sense of surprise when hearing one female passenger reveal that she hadn't noticed the bus was any different – to many, a bus is a bus, but one could surely distinguish between a pink Optare Solo and a red London double decker – New Routemaster or not! The trial presented Ipswich Buses with the opportunity to show its passengers how bus design was evolving, but the company has no intentions to operate New Routemasters. Indeed, Malcolm Robson remains to be convinced that current hybrid buses are commercially worthwhile.

So the Ipswich trial didn't lead to any conclusions that the type is well suited or otherwise for non-London use. It does perhaps highlight the different attitudes and demands of bus users across the country, and makes clear that efforts by manufacturers to enhance the outward appearance of buses may not always strike a chord with all passengers.

In July 2012, the Department for Transport announced its support for local authority-led proposals to introduce trolleybuses to Leeds. The proposals, jointly promoted by Leeds City Council and the city's transport authority, Metro, are referred to as the Leeds New Generation Transport (NGT) trolleybus system. The NGT system would extend over a distance of 14.8km, running between Holt Park in north-west of Leeds via the city centre to Stourton in the south east.

Two decades after the introduction of the UK's first low floor buses, the focus of manufacturers and operators alike had moved from vehicle accessibility to vehicle emissions and efficiency. Regardless of their opinion as to the most practical means of powering the bus of the future, most people would accept that the days of conventional diesel-only propulsion are numbered. Importantly though, from a passenger perspective, it will not matter how a bus is powered if the key objective of service reliability cannot be met.

In response to NGT, First Group developed proposals of its own to incorporate at least some of the key features of the New Routemaster, including the offer of multiple-door simultaneous boarding and smart-card ticketing. First also proposed to work in partnership with relevant local authorities to focus on known areas of traffic congestion, introducing measures which would reduce delays to local bus services.

By summer 2014 New Routemaster LT2, having returned from its global tour, was painted all-over green and then branded and vinyled for Leeds. LT2's visit to Leeds helped to launch First's consultation on what by that point was named a "New Bus for West Yorkshire" (NBfWY). First's consultation sought the views

LT2 arrived at Hunslet Park on 22nd July in all-over green. The special vinyls were added locally. The bus did not operate in public service at any time during its stay with First, but was put on display at many locations and also, showing a variety of blind displays, used for free rides at an open day at the Dewsbury museum in Ravensthope on 16th November, as seen in two views on this spread. The bus was also shown by First Group to officials from a number of local councils. The company's counter-proposal to the Leeds trolleybus scheme was based on a three-door bus to speed up boarding, coupled with bus priority measures, Oyster-style smartcards and greener technology.

of politicians, local businesses and members of the general public. The last public consultation took place in Leeds on 19th December, with the company having received useful feedback on what people liked and disliked about the bus. Specific questions asked by First included ones relating to the number of staircases, air-conditioning, opening windows, seating and on-board WiFi. Although some were in favour of air-conditioning, this would add about 1 tonne to the weight of the bus; this would require a third axle on the New Routemaster if that were the bus chosen.

The cover of the public consultation leaflet and LT2 seen leaving Huddersfield bus station where it had been on display.

Above left: Sir Brian Souter driving the first journey of LT312 (Stagecoach vehicle number 61312) on 3rd November. The two buses were the first New Routemasters to be registered as new by an operator other than TfL. They were registered in the name of Fife Scottish Omnibuses Ltd.

On 23rd October 2014 Stagecoach East Scotland announced that two New Routemasters would be tried out on its two-person operated route 73/73A in Dundee for three months from the beginning of November. They were for evaluation prior to Stagecoach possibly buying some of them in spring 2015. It was also an opportunity for Stagecoach to evaluate the three-door layout on a busy service, which operates between Abroath to the north east of Dundee and Ninewells Hospital in the west of the city. LTs 312 and 313, based at Stagecoach's Arbroath depot, entered service on Monday 3rd November, with Stagecoach chairman Sir Brian Souter driving the first bus in service. It was made clear to local people, in adverts and posters, that the company was trying out new technology but passengers suffered late running or cancellation of journeys which tried some people's patience. Within a week, the buses were 'temporarily withdrawn'. The main problems were insufficient battery power and unreliable operation of the rear doors. Later in November, the New Routemasters were relegated to unscheduled extras and shortly after the trial was abandoned. About the same time Stagecoach announced that a vintage Routemaster from the Stagecoach West Scotland heritage fleet would be running on the route from 8th December until Christmas Eve, with fares raised donated to a local charity. A week later the two New Routemasters were despatched to London.

Hourly journeys on routes 73 and 73A were scheduled on Mondays to Fridays, with buses setting off from Dundee city centre between 8.54 and 5.54. A less regular interval service with eight journeys was scheduled on Saturdays and there was no service with the buses on Sundays. The operating problems with the two buses were attributed locally to the long non-stop runs from the depot to the start of the route and further pressures being placed on the batteries by poor weather conditions.

Poster inside LTs 312 and 313 during their brief use in Dundee.

Now, a bit of imagination. Some readers might be familiar with a feature that appeared as an April Fool's item in Buses magazine for April 2013. The message behind the light-hearted story on that occasion was that there might well be other applications beyond TfL's for the vehicle and design. Further developing that idea, the computer generated images included on this spread show how the bus might look in other liveries and configurations. When the bus was first unveiled it was envisaged that it might be produced in different lengths and even open top versions and single deckers were not ruled out, though the former now has been and the latter seems unlikely with newer technologies imminent. Although these drawings are playful fantasy, a two door version of the bus seems likely.

UK operators have long been able to select chassis and bodywork combinations to suit their particular requirements. While bulk orders by the larger groups in recent years demonstrate examples of operators' favoured combinations, the development of relationships between chassis and body manufacturers means operators have fewer combinations from which to choose. As vehicle design continues to evolve, partnership working between operators and manufacturers will play an important role. This image gives an impression of how a New Routemaster might look if more conventional body and chassis examples were to be made available – in this case imagining bodywork added to a Volvo chassis and front cowl. Apologies to Ray Stenning for adapting his livery.

In August 2013, an LT visited the Anlaby Road premises of East Yorkshire Motor Services in Hull. The bus was not used in service but did feature in a television documentary about that company's operations. EYMS has a large fleet of a Wright buses, with both Gemini 1 and Gemini 2 examples in its fleet. This image shows a New Routemaster in the livery of Hull Corporation, which complements the curved appearance of the bodywork.

As covered in the previous spread, Stagecoach was able to use two buses on its two-man Dundee service 73 that were being stored ahead of their entry into service in London. That being the case, it is unlikely that there was ever any prospect that the trial buses would carry anything other than London red, but this image shows how Stagecoach group livery might appear if applied to a New Routemaster. The 73 branding is as applied to the fleet of Enviro 400s which, at that time, were assigned to the route.

Brighton & Hove might have been one of the companies taking up the New Routemaster if the bus had found favour outside London, though the present management have ruled it out. The very attractive B&H livery, another of Ray Stenning's, would have suited the bus in other circumstances.

ADIDAS AND OTHER ADS

JAMES WHITING

As another part of TfL's Year of the Bus, commemorating in its own words 'the centenary of the first mass-produced motor bus and the 60th anniversary of the RM', a number of LTs were given all-over advertisements. The great majority of these were for Adidas, who booked 32 black painted LTs that entered service starting on Saturday 24th May 2014. The advertising was part of its World Cup campaign and the number 32 represented the number of teams taking part in the tournament. It was announced that the advert buses would run for four months. Black is not a particularly flattering colour for the design and there were also concerns that it would make the interiors of the buses warmer than they otherwise would be. As interior temperatures varied between the new buses in any case, it was difficult to gauge whether this was so. If the cooling system was working effectively, the livery should have made no difference. The LTs were painted black before delivery and given the adverts in London, following which 25 of them (LTs 184-186, 191-194, 199, 201, 203-206, 209, 210, 213-215, 218-222, 233 and 238) were sent to Clapton for route 38 and seven (LTs 252-255 and 268-270) to Bow for route 8.

LTs 233 and 194 meet in New Oxford Street and show the mix of black paint and vinyls to create the Adidas advertising.

LT253 at Heysham Ferry, where it has arrived following its trip across the Irish Sea, awaiting its drive down south for the vinyls to be added.

Vinyls depicting one of four footballers were applied to the offside of each bus: Uruguay's Luis Suarez, England's Steven Gerrard, Germany's Mesut Ozil and Brazil's Dani Alves. Four different slogans were carried: 'all in or nothing' (ten buses), 'fear or be feared' (ten), 'now or never' (six) and 'hunt or be hunted' (six). Following Luis Suarez biting an opponent in the World Cup game between Uruguay and Italy, he was disowned by Adidas and on 28th June was peeled off the LTs on which he appeared. England's worst ever World Cup performance also led to Steven Gerrard coming off the buses soon after. In contrast, buses carrying a photo of Mesut Ozil had four gold stars added to reflect the World Cup being won by Germany.

LT219 against a backdrop of banners for the Year of the Bus parade in Regent Street on the morning of Sunday 21st June 2014.

A set of views when the buses were new into service shows the application of the advertising around the buses. Up to this point, all-over advertising had been ruled out for the LTs but some of the revenue from these was used to support the Year of the Bus, whose sponsors included Exterion Media and Arriva.

adidas
38
Cyclists
Stay back
available at:
adidas
white city, oxford street. stratford.
adidas.com/worldcup
LTZ 1215

A minority of the Adidas buses carried the TfL Buses roundel, as seen on LT269 on the last N8 journey to Hainault one morning in June and also LT268 after losing its footballer. In contrast, LT221 might give the impression to some passengers that Adidas is the operator. LTs featuring Germany's Mesut Ozil had the 'or nothing' blanked out and four gold stars added following his team's World Cup record 7-1 win against Brazil.

Half way through the four-month contract, a new design began to appear on the Adidas buses. In the first view, the new vinyls are being applied by Exterion Media (previously CBS Outdoor) staff inside Clapton garage. Each bus's set of vinyls took four or five men between six and eight hours to apply, so one bus was done per day. The advertising on all the vinyls in this style carried the same wording as shown on LTs 184 and 269.

LT192 appeared on 13th August with a completely different Adidas advert to publicise the opening of their new flagship store in Fouberts Place off Carnaby Street. This used the Adidas stripes but had a strangely amateurish look compared to the earlier schemes. The bus is seen on its second day at work in the new livery at Hyde Park Corner and later in its contract at Victoria.

During its very short period in Coca-Cola livery, LT148 is seen at King's Cross and Oxford Circus. The front of the bus was in standard livery. This was in effect a prototype for future all-over adverts as consideration was being given at the time to the possibility that future such contracts could employ vinyls on the basic red livery to avoid the complications of repainting buses into red livery after the end of the term of the contract. This idea evolved into having advert buses painted all-over white, on which advert vinyls could easily be changed without a full repaint into another colour.

At the other end of the scale of advertising exposure was Coca-Cola, who had one bus in overall livery for a very short time. Described by Coca-Cola in advertising jargon as 'a one-off activation', LT148 ran in service from Stamford Brook garage for just a few days in the second week of June with Coca-Cola vinyls applied to standard red livery. Then in mid-August LT100 was given vinyls for Fender guitars in a contract that was scheduled to run until the end of the year (though extended due to the bus being out of action for just over a month following an accident). There was also a short lived pink LT but this was painted red before it left Northern Ireland and it did not carry an all-over advert. LT230 was painted pink for the Giro D'Italia cycle race, which has become associated with the colour and whose leading cyclist wears a pink jersey.

LT100 was unveiled on 19th August with vinyls for the famous Fender Stratocaster electric guitars. A limited edition of twenty-five Fender Routemaster red and cream guitars featuring the RM seat moquette pattern was manufactured by the company, one of which was offered as a prize in a competition open to unsigned bands. The advert bus entered service the following day from Holloway garage for use on routes 24, passing near the Jazz Cafe and the Roundhouse in Camden Town and also Denmark Street, and 390, passing the 100 Club in Oxford Street. The red at the front of the bus was a little lighter than in standard livery and the registration number recess was framed in black. Fender has produced a wide range of special editions of its guitars and this was one of a number celebrating its 60th anniversary. The first Stratocaster was designed by Leo Fender in 1954, when the original Routemaster first appeared. The London Transport Museum's Nadia Adira holds one of the guitars offered at a retail price of £899. LT100 was involved in an accident on the morning of the 12th October smashing its windscreen. It was out of service for over a month.

And still they came. Further all over adverts on LTs appeared in September and October, with steadily deteriorating taste. First Red Bull on six buses in connection with a rock music event at Earls Court, then YouTube on another six. These were followed by a particularly unattractive scheme for Ugg Boots. Boris Johnson expressed his distaste for the New Routemaster all-over adverts – mentioning Red Bull by name – at the November TfL Board Meeting. Leon Daniels – referring to the necessary financing of the Year of the Bus – assured him at the meeting that all would be back to normal at the end of the year. Heatherwick made no comment, but it is difficult to imagine the Studio being happy with them either.

At the start of 2015 a few Adidas liveried LTs were still running, but a repaint programme was well progressed. Stratocaster LT100 was also still running, but Fender were owed a month following its accident. Apart from these, the all-over ads were the plainer white-based ones first seen on the YouTube buses in September 2014.

The last new all-over advert of 2014 was for Android software in November, seen in these views of LTs 53 and 55. It was the first example of white buses getting a change of all-over advert – previously YouTube was carried on these.

UGG
Hammersmith 9
UGG
australia
PICCADILLY KNIGHTSBRIDGE COVENT GARDEN WESTFIELD LONDON
This Is UGG.
LTZ 1077

UGG
australia
This Is UGG.
PICCADILLY KNIGHTSBRIDGE COVENT GARDEN WESTFIELD LONDON

COMPETITION – FIVE YEARS ON

ALAN MILLAR

Five years after the 2009 manufacturers' competition, there were four new double-deck bus designs on the market and it is worth comparing these with the New Routemaster. In addition to the Volvo B5TL/Wright Gemini 3 and Mercedes-powered Wright StreetDeck, two other new Euro VI-engined double-deckers were launched in May 2014, both targeted at the London market as well as beyond. These were the all-new Alexander Dennis Enviro400 and the first-ever integral double-decker from Optare, the MetroDecker.

Although derived from the previous Enviro400 and using the same aluminium structure, the Euro VI model from ADL is substantially different with far more chassis parts in common with the company's next generation single-deckers than was the case before. It benefits from a thorough redesign of potential failure items in the chassis and body, as the manufacturer analysed the warranty records for all of the Enviro400 and Trident double-deckers it had supplied since 2006, seeking solutions to problems these will have thrown up. At its launch, Alexander Dennis was claiming a net weight saving of 400kg over the Euro V version, after allowing for the additional exhaust after treatment required to maintain the new emissions levels. It will be offered in three lengths and two heights, those for London being the 'highbridge' version of 4.3m (14ft 1in); it hopes to fit 70 seats and two doors into the shortest, 10.2m, model for London.

A London specification Enviro400 on display in the Alexander Dennis headquarters at Larbert.

Mechanically, it differs from all its Euro VI competitors in pure diesel form by retaining a six-cylinder engine, the 6.7litre Cummins ISB. Hybrids will use the Chinese-built four-cylinder version as fitted in the New Routemaster. Styling was a priority for Alexander Dennis, which – like Wrightbus with its new models – was keen to take some front-end styling cues from its previous successful design. Although there is a resemblance, especially in the shape of the top deck windscreen, the parts are different. The rear, with black mouldings encapsulating the windows from both decks and sculpted 'hips' around the engine compartment covers, is intended to make this double-decker look a little more like a luxury coach.

A new quick release glazing system combines the appearance of bonded glazing with the replacement speed of rubber gasket glazing, which several London operators have continued to specify. Alexander Dennis says a damaged window can be removed and replaced within 6 minutes, all achieved from the inside of the bus without requiring potentially unsafe lifting platforms. As one of the leading suppliers of London double-deckers, Alexander Dennis is counting on this new model at very least helping it maintain its share of this market.

For Optare, with no integral double decker available previously and modest single-deck sales in London (mainly to RATP fleets), every sale will be a conquest. Its unique sales proposition is the weight of the MetroDecker, which at 9,980kg on the London-specification prototype is the best part of a tonne lighter than any of its rivals. It says it has achieved this by use of a stainless steel rather than aluminium structure as on its single-deckers but not found on any UK double-deckers for over 20 years – and by building it as a true integral without any unnecessary weight. In this latter respect it owes something to the original Routemaster.

The prototype Optare MetroDecker is to London specification and was launched at the London Transport Museum in Covent Garden. This view shows it at the NEC. In a possibly unguarded moment, a senior Optare manager told bus journalists at the launch of the MetroDecker in May 2014 that, in standard diesel form, a London-specification model would have a price tag of around £210,000. We can take it that its rivals will be selling for similar sums. Electric hybrids are estimated to be about £110,000 more expensive to buy than their diesel equivalents, putting the price of a London example within touching distance of the price of a New Routemaster.

Like the StreetDeck, it has a four-cylinder Mercedes-Benz OM934LA engine, but this is mounted transversely with an angle-drive. Wrightbus argues that the engine is short enough to be mounted in-line in the StreetDeck, with a T-drive arrangement saving fuel. Optare argues that the MetroDecker layout gives it the shortest possible rear overhang (2,390mm) and that there is no fuel penalty with an angle-drive. Optare has packaged the heating and ventilation system above the engine compartment, leaving the MetroDecker with a smaller lower deck back window than the Alexander Dennis and Wrightbus vehicles.

At 10.5m, the MetroDecker is slightly longer than the Enviro400 and the same length as the Gemini 3/StreetDeck in standard form. However, at 2.5m it is slightly narrower than all the other new generation double-deckers, which are 2.55m wide. This makes it comply with the current width limit in Australia and New Zealand, where Optare hopes to secure export sales. It says the thinner steel structure means it is only fractionally narrower inside than other UK double-deckers, a claim that could be put to the test if its lower weight translates into a higher permitted standing capacity, as Optare believes it could accommodate between 36 and 53 standees in a 63-seat London layout. The centre door is slightly farther back than on other double-deckers, placing it directly opposite the wheelchair bay. Most of the side glazing is bonded, but Optare plans to offer its version of a quick release system on the lower deck windows. The system will be accessed from the outside, as are all chassis maintenance points, thus reducing the risk of fitters' dirty boots soiling the flooring.

Visually, the MetroDecker is the least curved of all the new double-deckers. While clearly a modern bus, its flat sides, angular corners and raked front give it a shape reminiscent of a wartime utility bus, albeit one clad in composites with curved mouldings. Inside, the staircase panel is illuminated from behind a false window. Optare plans to offer hybrid and all-electric versions in 2015. Given its leadership in the small, but emerging, market for electric single-deckers, this could be the edge it needs to establish itself in an already crowded market.

Can the competition learn something from the New Routemaster? Even if the New Routemaster remains a bus exclusively for London, its influence could spread farther, in particular to other bus interiors – in London and beyond. Among the weaknesses that Heatherwick Studio identified in existing bus designs were staircases and seats. By glazing the staircases of the New Routemaster, it sought to make this into a positive and welcoming feature, inviting passengers to use it to reach the upper deck and not feel as though they were being condemned to climb inside a dimly lit tunnel. Many may initially have dismissed this extra glazing as quirky – even as unnecessary additional weight – but if they appreciate its purpose they could surely be persuaded to specify it on other vehicles.

Besides Lothian's adoption of a glazed staircase on its Gemini 3s, Optare has taken some heed of this lesson by fitting a false window with back lighting on the MetroDecker. These could be the first signs of a developing trend. The seats could be next. Heatherwick's people dismissed the crop of contemporary bus seats – standard products from a range of international manufacturers – as little better than those in rally cars. Most are moulded in plastic with varying levels of upholstery, but none of it comparable with what Londoners – and many others – enjoyed on the likes of a Routemaster or RT, even if air suspension neutralises some of

Stagecoach was one of the first customers for the Wright Gemini 3-bodied Volvo B5LH hybrid, taking 32 for the Selkent fleet in London. The upper deck windows without openers are just three-quarters of an inch deeper than those on the LTs.

the effect of poor road surfaces. Even the bench seats upstairs on provincial lowbridge double-deckers of 50 to 60 years ago had accommodatingly comfortable cushions. Heatherwick saw this as part of a trend to make buses fit around what was available on an industrial scale rather than what passengers might prefer to use. The studio fought hard to develop a better seat, something that blends a modern structure into a design that looks – and, crucially, feels – more like a traditional two-person seat. Having developed the seat for the New Routemaster, there is an opportunity to make it available for other buses, as an alternative to seats which in many cases were developed for continental single-deckers on which the majority of peak period passengers stand. So, while the overall shape and layout of the New Routemaster may remain unique to that vehicle, it could have a profound influence on some key areas of other bus designs.

Lothian Buses took a batch of Gemini 3s in late 2014 that were the first to incorporate staircase glazing.

AT HOME IN LONDON

GAVIN BOOTH

You will rarely read the words 'sensuous curves' in a transport book, yet it is difficult not to be seduced by the rounded front and – even better – the wonderful rear view of a New Routemaster. Even though these buses are an increasingly common sight in central London and beyond, it is difficult not to smile when you see them and marvel at the speed Wrightbus has been building them. Compared with the 'old' Routemaster, which had a longer gestation period – almost five years from the first public appearance of RM1 in 1954 to the first buses entering service in quantity late in 1959 – there were just 20 months between the unveiling in Ballymena and the conversion of the 24 route in June 2013.

Transport for London is in a strong position to dictate what kind of buses run on its massive network. Although it only owns a very small proportion of the 7,500 buses providing its comprehensive service pattern, it does dictate where these buses should go, and when, and what fares it charges its growing band of over 2 billion customers annually.

London orders account for a significant proportion of new full-size bus deliveries and manufacturers have become well used to designing or adapting models with more than half an eye to orders from the contractors providing London services, which led observers around the country to pose the question: did we really need the Boris Bus?

London had led the move towards low-floor buses in the mid-1990s, and powered ahead to achieve an all-accessible fleet by 2005, save for the Heritage Routemasters. It had started with small batches of low-floor single-deckers, bodied by Wrights in Ballymena, then a relatively minor player in the UK bus-building scene. When low-floor double-deckers came on line, London operators invested heavily in these and a London specification emerged, built by a range of bodybuilders on a number of different chassis types. Although these were Londonised buses, they were usually not too different from deliveries to operators in the rest of the country.

The main chassis suppliers were, initially DAF and Dennis, soon to be joined by Volvo and later by Scania, typically with bodywork by Alexander, East Lancs, Plaxton, Scania or Wrights. Subsequent ownership changes brought Alexander, Dennis and Plaxton together as Alexander Dennis, East Lancs into the Optare fold, and DAF's buses now carry the VDL name.

Although they are externally identical to double-deckers supplied to operators around the UK, the London deliveries incorporate features rarely seen elsewhere, like a separate exit door, and as a consequence of this a relatively low number of lower deck seats. Where a 10.4m-long Volvo B9TL/Wright Gemini in Go-Ahead's London fleet has seats for just 62 passengers, a single-door example in the same group's Brighton & Hove company has 71 seats with 28 rather than just 21 on the lower deck, with more provision for less able passengers.

A contrast in tail-ends – from the left an Enviro400, a Wrightbus Gemini and a New Routemaster, complete with 'sensuous curves'.

The specification of London's off-the-peg double-deckers has evolved and while passengers from other parts of the UK may find the interior layout unfamiliar to them, it is clearly what TfL deems necessary for London's apparently unique operating conditions. A separate exit door makes a great deal of sense in speeding up passenger flow, yet outside London even the most fervent advocates of two-door buses have reluctantly moved to a single door layout, usually citing the increase in the number of exit door accidents and insurance claims; a proportion of these are spurious, but the cost of dealing with these has driven most urban operators back to single doors.

The low seating capacity in the lower deck of London buses has been a bone of contention with passengers, particularly those who are looking for a seat on the low-floor section rather than climbing up on to a pedestal-mounted seat. The lack of low-floor seats – indeed many seats at all – does not seem passenger-friendly. And the lower deck layout is not always helped by what seems to be a particularly London habit, inspired perhaps by Tube travellers, of passengers crowding round the centre door making it difficult for other passengers to alight.

A Boris Bus T-shirt and a fridge magnet.

The most familiar off-the-peg buses on London's streets today, the ADL Enviro400 and the Volvo/Wrightbus Gemini, are attractive and distinctive products, but represent evolution rather than the revolution that is New Routemaster. Alexander Dennis and Volvo have been the main suppliers of London's growing fleet of diesel-electric hybrid double-deckers and have had the most to lose as TfL received its deliveries of LTs.

Although I must admit I was more than a little sceptical when I first heard about the bus we have now come to know as the New Routemaster, it has won me over. It looks very much at home in London as did the 'old' Routemasters and RTs before it. It offers passengers a quiet, pleasant ride on comfortable 'proper' seats with excellent vision from both decks, even from the shallow upper deck windows that some have criticised. It is disappointing to see New Routemasters in overall advertising liveries, but income is income. The buses can get a bit hot and stuffy but the air chill system seemed to be working better on hot days in June 2014 than when I first experienced them on the 38 and 24 a year earlier.

Photos comparing the upper deck interior of a Gemini body (left) with the New Routemaster.

New Routemasters galore in Whitehall traffic. Note how the New Routemaster front dome echoes the curved top of the telephone box on the right.

The driver of LT23 negotiates the left turn at St George's Square, Pimlico where the traffic island was moved one metre off centre to allow the new buses to make this manoeuvre. The next longest double-deckers in TfL service are the Scania OmniCitys which are 10.8 metres. Most Gemini 2s are 10.4 metres long and the Enviro400s 10.1 metres.

The long wheelbase and the overall length of 11.3m mean that some tight turns on several of the New Routemaster routes require careful negotiation, and nobody would pretend that the New Routemaster could ever be as nippy as its distinguished Routemaster predecessor, although its speed between stops on straight roads is impressive where traffic allows.

There has been much mumbling about the cost of the New Routemaster, at £354,000 each, which for a bus bristling with new features is not a great deal more than an off-the-peg hybrid. The development costs of around £11million were used mischievously by some to suggest that the eight prototypes were costing £1.375million each, and if the bus had been stillborn at this stage there might have been some justification, but every manufacturer incurs development costs for each new model and these are recouped from subsequent sales. When you consider the long gestation period of the Routemaster, TfL, the designers and Wrightbus did remarkably well to take the New Routemaster from an idea to full production in just three years.

For passengers, most importantly, it seems to be a success. Passengers I spoke to on the 24 liked the look and feel of the LTs and visitors and locals alike enjoyed the chance to use the open rear platform at stops and when the bus was caught in traffic. I am happy to admit that I am a convert to the New Routemaster. From initial scepticism – why do they need this when ADL and Volvo can supply perfectly good hybrids? – I was won over by the way the bus looks, the ride, the interior décor, and feel that TfL, Heatherwick Studios and Wrightbus have combined to produce an important new type for London – maybe just for London so far as the UK is concerned, though I would guess some of its design features might appear on other buses. By the middle of the century London's then mayor will probably be under pressure to develop an equally iconic successor.

Another fridge magnet featured one of the competition entries, albeit shown the wrong way round. This design was also to be seen on a T-shirt.

Aside from the arguments one way or the other regarding the cost, suitability and value of the new bus, it has quickly become part of the London landscape and its beautiful shape is almost universally admired. The routes chosen for the first 200 or so buses have contributed to its high profile. Tourist spots the buses passed in their first year of volume service include Trafalgar Square, Parliament Square, St Paul's, Hyde Park, Marble Arch, Westminster Bridge, Camden Town and Oxford Street.

15
TRAFALGAR SQUARE
CAN SOMEONE GET ME A TICKET?
Liverpool Street

THE CUMBERLAND
Notting Hill Gate 390
Metroline
"I ♥ MORMON"
LTZ 1033

White City 148
LONDON UNITED
Smart picks from over a million properties.
Zoopla
LTZ 1123

BORIS BUS SCULPTURES

JAMES WHITING

In July 2014 it was announced that a 'Year of the Bus' sculpture event would be mounted in the autumn. Various organisations had previously staged sculpture trails of things like eggs, elephants and telephone boxes in London and elsewhere. The bus sculptures were the idea of TfL's Intellectual Property Rights Manager David Ellis and were taken forward by TfL's Year of the Bus Project Manager Jon Hodges. Inspired partly by the Cow Parade sculptures held most years in cities around the world and partly by the 2012 Olympic mascots, the project soon enlisted the help of Wild in Art, a creative events company that has been promoting public art since it was formed in 2007. Artists interested in taking part were invited to submit ideas and about 100 up-and-coming or established artists expressed a wish to participate.

After a special event at the London Transport Museum on 16th July, at which 75 potential designs were shown to potential sponsors, about 40 drawings were selected to be progressed to sculpture buses, work on these taking place between August and early October.

Kristjana S Williams was commissioned to do two buses for the Westminster trail, one sponsored by the Metro newspaper and displayed at the foot of Charing Cross Road and the other sponsored by Cubic and displayed outside TfL's Windsor House headquarters in Victoria Street. The latter was one of a small number of sculptures displayed in adjacent empty shop units at 55 Broadway, as seen here, prior to the full launch.

Each artist was asked to first to submit a drawing of their proposed work for approval. This example is from Pawel Srokowski who won first prize at the event held at the London Transport Museum in July to sign up sponsors. For this design it was originally intended to reuse broken mirrors but this approach was deemed unsafe, so polycarbonate material was used instead. In this phase of the project, Pawel was joined by his wife Ewelina and the photo shows work in progress. The final result was put in position in front of the Olympic Stadium in Stratford as illustrated on page 193. Many of the artists worked in their own studios, homes or garages while others had the use of other studio premises, including a disused railway arch at Shepherd's Bush.

Liverpool based artist Stephen McKay worked on a design inspired by the Dazzle camouflage invented by artists for ships in the first world war. Over 2000 ships were painted – each differently – in such camouflage, which worked by making it difficult to estimate a target's range, speed and direction. Prior to going on display near HMS Belfast between London Bridge and Tower Bridge it appeared at an Acton Depot open weekend.

Trafalgar Square on the morning of 17th October, where the press launch of the sculpture buses has also attracted a number of passers-by and people who have heard about it on London local radio.

Following a showcase of some of the bus sculptures at the shop unit that had been used as a studio at 55 Broadway, the trail was launched to the media at Trafalgar Square on Friday 17th October when 28 of a planned 60 buses, 2.5m long, 1m high and 0.5m wide, were put on display in autumn morning sunshine. The total of 60 celebrated the 60th birthday of the original Routemaster. Each fibreglass sculpture weighs about 65kg and was mounted on a 450kg concrete-filled plinth. TfL and Wild in Art worked with the GLA to temporarily instal overnight the maximum number that could be squeezed into Trafalgar Square so that people would stumble across them on their way to work and generate interest – which they certainly did. Mention was also made of the sculptures on London local radio.

The stated aims for the trail were to promote walking, to highlight the vital role the bus plays in the capital and, chiefly, to raise money for charity. The charities to benefit, by way of an auction, were Kid's Company, overseas development charity Transaid and the London Transport Museum. £900 was paid to artists for each bus and the statues were placed in an on-line auction with an initial minimum bid of £3000 (later reduced to £1000). The siting and positioning of the sculptures was decided in consultation with the relevant local authorities with sponsors' preferences taken into account.

Two of the sculptures were in their allocated place at the time of the launch, one at the top of Whitehall and one next to St Martin in the Fields in Charing Cross Road. The following day, 15 more were put in place in Westminster in a trail that started in Victoria Street, opposite Westminster Cathedral, and ended at the London Transport Museum, passing the TfL Headquarters at Windsor House on the way. On the Sunday another 11 appeared in or around the City of London, plus two outside the London Buses headquarters at Palestra House opposite Southwark Underground station. On the Monday it was the turn of the area in and around the Queen Elizabeth Olympic Park, Stratford. Eleven were put on display here.

Rob Wilson was one of a minority of artists who knew in advance where his bus would be placed. He was approached at the beginning of August to do something for the traffic island between Nelson's column and the top of Whitehall and he decided on a 360 degree panorama of the views from that position. It was one of two buses put in place neighbouring Trafalgar Square for the launch and the only bus to have a New Routemaster painted on it. The second view shows Rob at work on the bus in his studio. The bus models were based on a mesh frame covered in fibreglass covered in plaster. At the conclusion of the Trafalgar Square press display, the buses – each weighing about 80kgs – are forklifted onto trucks. Sophie Green's Dazzler bus, based on wartime boat camouflage and sponsored by Metroline, was destined for the Olympic Park where it was put in place on the following Monday.

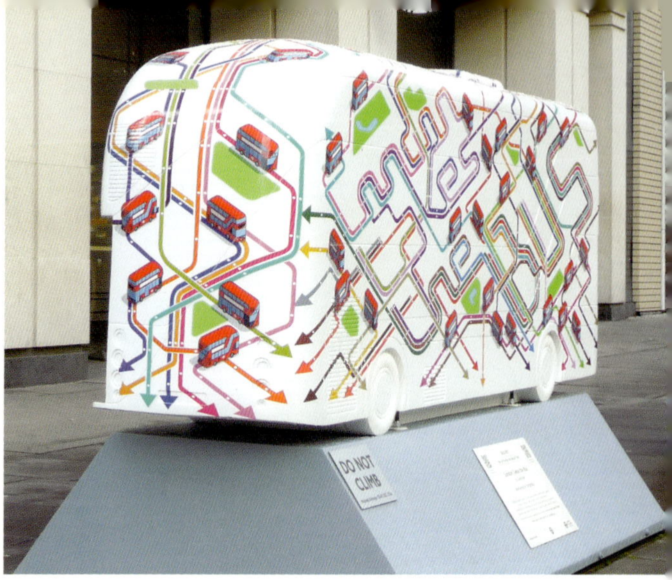

Above left: This design by Jenny Leonard was placed outside Westminster City Hall and, by request, remained in place after all the others had been moved.

Above: Inspired by the Central London Bus Map, Rod Hunt used lines representing bus routes to spell out the title of his work 'London Takes the Bus'. It was one of five painted bus sculptures put on display in Victoria Street.

Centre: 'Lest we Forget' was another bus to commemorate the 100th anniversary of the first world war and to remember those who died fighting in it. Designed by Lee O'Brien, it was placed opposite Horse Guards in Whitehall and is seen being viewed on Remembrance Sunday.

Five telephone boxes formed the design painted on another of Stephen McKay's buses (see also the Dazzle bus), and was placed alongside one of Giles Gilbert Scott's originals in Parliament Square.

Above: The basement of the Long Acre branch of Stanfords, well-known for maps, atlases and travel guides, was the place to find 'Travels with Edward' by Valerie Osment. The design was inspired by Edward Stanford's *Library Map of London*, published in 1862, recognised as the first accurate map of London ever produced, and shows sketches that might have been done by a visitor to London using the map as a guide, plus pages from the *Illustrated London News* of the time.

Left: Sian Storey produced this colourful tribute to 1960s 'Swinging London' which was to be found in St Martin's Court.

Two buses were placed alongside the entrance to the London Transport Museum, 'Busby' by Oliver Dean and 'Accessibus' by Lilianna Garza. Busby had a top that sought to reflect the military fur hats worn by the Queen's Guard, but made of a hardwearing material to withstand the inevitable tactile attention. Accessibus invited people to add, in chalk, their ideas about accessibility related to buses.

Top: Two buses were placed outside the entrance to Palestra House, the headquarters of London Buses, 'New Routemaster' by Candida Boyes and 'Legible London' by Fiona Stewart, a celebration of street signage. The plain red New Routemaster was not placed in the auction but retained by LBSL.

Above: 'Spectrum' – a kaleidoscopic collection of colour – by Liverpool-based artist Kristel Pillkahn was placed alongside Glaziers Hall, neighbouring the river, and was one of ten sponsored by Cubic Transportation Systems. Kristel's studio partner Sophie Green decorated two other bus sculptures.

Left: 'Route Masters' is being inspected by a couple of visitors to the Bankside area, who may well be trying to identify all the characters on the design by Edward Carvalho-Monaghan. Eight figures are repeated around the bus, including Sherlock Holmes, a pharaoh, a beefeater and a Chelsea Pensioner.

Above and left: 'Twenty Four Seven' was designed to celebrate the 24-hour service provided by London buses and was sponsored by Abellio. On one side is a daytime and sunset view and on the other a night-time and sunrise scene. Deven Bhurke used a wide range of colours to convey the vibrant life of London. Tower Bridge also featured on a design by Michelle Heron, which was sited next to the old Billingsgate fish market.

Above: Another, and contemporary, take on the first world war dazzle camouflage, this one incorporating the roundel, was produced by Sophie Green. In comparison with the one shown on page 185 (also by a Liverpool based artist), this one was painted in various colours. Sophie Green also did two other buses.

Left: 'Hold Tight' used reproductions of Bell Punch and Gibson bus tickets. It was designed by Mini Moderns, who usually specialise in interior design products such as wallpapers, fabrics, cushions, rugs and ceramics. Clients include the London Transport Museum

Below: 'English Herbaceous Border' by Sarah Jane Richards features plants that have been used in formal gardens since the Victorian era – Peonie, Phlox, Schizostyliss and Coreopsis – all drawn in the style of traditional botanical illustrations.

Above: 'The Paralympic Bus' was one of 11 sculptures placed in the Queen Elizabeth Olympic Park at Stratford. It was painted by mouth in two weeks of eight hour days by artist Tom Yendell, born without arms owing to the drug Thalidomide, taken by pregnant women in the early 1960s to relieve morning sickness. The sculpture is seen in front of the Orbit and the Olympic Stadium.

Left: Children take a close look at the 'Invisible to the Environment' bus referred to earlier in connection with its winning first prize at the sponsors' event at the LT Museum. It is clear here why polycarbonate was used to cover the bus rather than the originally planned broken glass.

Below: Loz (short for Laura) Atkinson drew on a life-long fascination with clouds as inspiration for her CumulonimBUS. Loz was previously involved in similar sculpture projects involving eggs, elephants, hornbills and telephone boxes.

Somewhat isolated from the other bus sculptures was 'Come Rain or Come Shine' by Thomas Dowdeswell. Sponsored by the Highways Agency, it was sited in the Edgware Road halfway between Marble Arch and the Marylebone Flyover and on the one route through central London that is exempt from the congestion charge. Its designer, Thomas Dowdeswell, has become well known for his 'Vortescapes', which he bases on Vorticism, Cubism and the Avant Garde and which he describes as darkly comic, frenetic, fictional tales of life in the city. The high degree of detail in the work is reflected in the time taken: seven 25-30-hour weeks – almost certainly more work than any other of the buses. In common with the designer of the Stanfords bus, Thomas had also produced a Bookbench for Wild in Art as part of another charity fundraising project earlier in 2014. Details on his bus include Cubist representations of seated passengers, bikes and trains whizzing across the scene and lines of commuters.

Arguably the most impressive of the sculpture buses, 'Come Rain or Come Shine' is seen in position at the junction of Nutford Place and Edgware Road. The passenger holding on to the hand rail at the rear door is a reference to the time when the artist's then girlfriend got hold of the pole on a Routemaster as it was pulling away.

A further 17 sculptures appeared in Croydon two weeks before Christmas, with all in place on Monday 8th December. The display locations had not been decided at the time the designs were invited, but it was anticipated that most would be in the town centre and this proved to be the case. The trail celebrated the identity, transport, history and future of Croydon with six of the 17 designs produced by local artists. On completion of this fourth trail the total of bus sculptures was 58, 57 of which were brought together next to the Aquatics Centre at the Queen Elizabeth Olympic Park in the second week of January 2015 ready for an open event on the weekend of 24th and 25th. Two other buses were on show there including one painted 'live' at the event by a group of artists on the weekend. Some buses had been removed from their sites in late December in locations that were going to be busy on New Year's Eve. The sculpture bus outside Westminster City Hall stayed in place for an extended period by request.

The Croydon buses were put in place over the weekend of 6th and 7th December with all being on display from the Monday. 'Diversity' by Rachel Stevens celebrates Croydon's history and wide variety of architecture. Rachel Stevens usually works in watercolours but, like most of the other bus artists, used durable acrylic paints for this project.

Above: Parked outside Croydon Council's Access House offices was 'Croydon Layers' which, like Rachel Stevens's work, included some architectural elements including the Whitgift Almshouses and the roof of the town hall. Two rows of local bus route numbers ran round the bus about half way up. Matt Bannister was the artist.

Left: 'Poppy the Party Bus' by Jenny Leonard was inspired by British sixties and seventies pop culture and aimed at reflecting London's vibrancy with a colourful and lively design that was placed in North End.

'Do the Locomotive' was to be seen at Reeves Corner where it was passed at frequent intervals by the local trams. On the offside of this design, by Anna Rawles and Jennifer Rodgers, was a steam locomotive. This partnership did three buses for the project: one other in Croydon and one in Threadneedle Street.

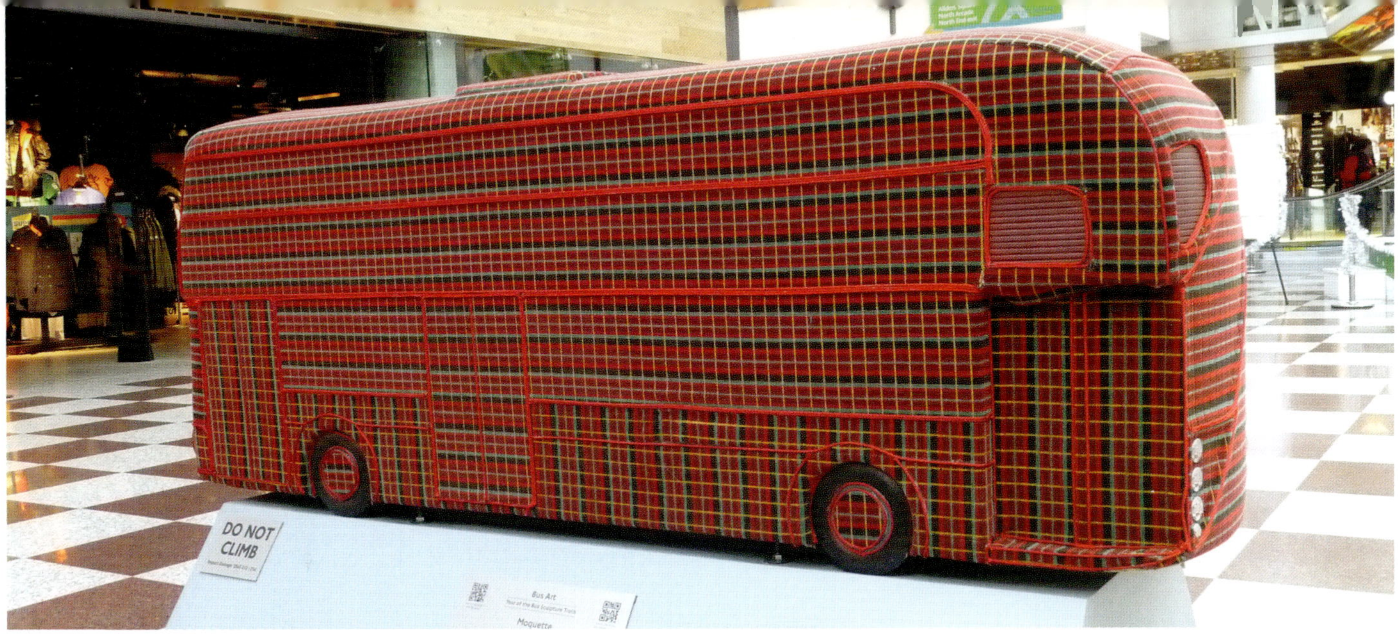

RM moquette covered one of three bus sculptures installed inside the Whitgift shopping centre. It was another design by Mini Moderns, but executed by Michele Pouncey. A preview of this bus had been available on the TfL stand at the Euro Bus Expo at Birmingham NEC between 4th and 6th November. Michele has experience in making soft props for children's television programmes including Bob the Builder and The Clangers. Because it was covered in wool, the bus was always displayed indoors, including on the Sculpture Bus Family weekend at Stratford in January. Two buses had the name Moquette, the second being a painted design with little similarity to any London pattern.

THE ARTISTS, SITING AND SPONSORS

WESTMINSTER

1 Accessibus
Liliana Ortega Garza
London Transport Museum
University College London

2 Busby
Oliver Dean
London Transport Museum
Equifax

3 Poppy Fields
Sarah Jane Grace
Covent Garden
Capco Covent Garden

4 Travels with Edward
Valerie Osment
Stanford's Long Acre
Edward Stanford

5 Swinging London
Sian Storey
St Martins
Cubic

6 Rock n Royal
Damien Jeffery
Leicester Square
Raphaels Bank

7 Cath Kidston London Scene
Cath Kidston
Piccadilly Circus
Cath Kidston

8 London Skyline Bus
Kristjana S Williams
Charing Cross Road
Metro

9 360° Panorama of London
Rob Wilson
Trafalgar Square
The Mayor of London

10 Lest We Forget
Lee O'Brien
Horse Guards Avenue
Go Ahead

11 London Telephone Bus
Stephen McKay
Parliament Street
Cubic

12 London Takes the Bus
Rod Hunt
Victoria Street
Wrightbus

13 Buckingham Palace Bus
Mandii Pope
Victoria Street
Cubic

14 Gull Graeni Straeto
Kristjana S Williams
Victoria Street
Cubic

15 Lord Mayor of the City of Westminster
Jenny Leonard
Victoria Street
Westminster City Council

16 Tunnel Vision
One Red Shoe
Cardinal Place
Land Securities

17 Come Rain or Come Shine
Thomas Dowdeswell
Edgware Road
London Highways Agency

'Tunnel Vision' was the first of the buses to receive an initial bid, one for £3000 being placed on-line on 17th January. It was also the one to achieve the highest final bid (£3500) of all the buses. Winning bids totalled £82,750.

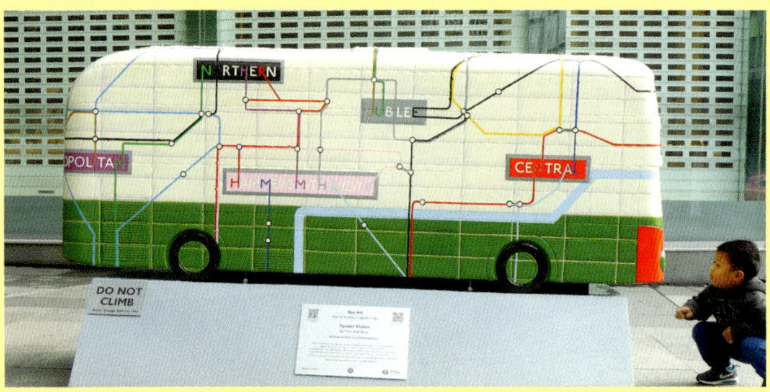

AROUND THE RIVER

1 Dazzle Bus
Stephen McKay
London Bridge City Pier
Cubic

2 Spectrum
Kristel Pillkahn
Glaziers Hall
Cubic

3 Orla Kiely
Sarah Jane Richards
St Mary Overie's Dock
Cubic

4 Route Masters
Edward Carvalho-Monaghan
Bankside
Cubic

5 Brollybus
Jane Veveris Callan
Bankside
Cubic

6 New Routemaster
Candida Boyes
Blackfriars Road
TfL Buses Directorate

7 Legible London
Fiona Stewart
Blackfriars Road
TfL Surface Transport

8 Punk'ed
Valerie Osment
St Paul's Cathedral Visitor Centre
Tesco

9 Childhood on a bus
Arizona Smith, ambassador for Kids Company
Friday Street
Mizuho

10 Push Once
Mini Moderns, painted by Sophie Green
Cheapside
Arriva

11 All Aboard the Number 8
Anna Rawles and Jennifer Rodgers
Threadneedle Street
Exterion Media

12 Tower Bridge Bus
Michelle Heron
Old Billingsgate – Thames Path
Asda

13 Twenty Four Seven
Deven Bhurke
Gloucester Close
Abellio

'All aboard the Number 8' featured places along route 8 and was sited on the route in Threadneedle Street.

OLYMPIC PARK

1 Ding! Ding!
Crispin Finn
International Square
Westfield

2 Moquette
Beth Quinton
East Village Visitors Centre
RATP Dev

3 Journey to Anywhere
Oliver Dean
Victory Park, East Village
Transport for London

4 Time Travel
Sara Adhitya
Timber Lodge Cafe
Clear Channel

5 English Herbaceous Border
Sarah Jane Richards
North of the Park
Unite

6 Hold Tight
Mini Moderns
painted by Jane Headford
North of the Park
Stagecoach

7 Union Jack
Kristian Movahed
Mandeville Place
Wild in Art

8 The Paralympic Bus
Tom Yendell
Mandeville Place
Cubic

9 Invisible to the Environment
Pawel Srokowski
South of the Park
Michelin Solutions

10 Dazzler
Sophie Green
Arcelor Mittal Orbit
Metroline

11 CumulonimBUS
Loz Atkinson
The International Quarter
The International Quarter

'Journey to Anywhere' was based on the London Underground map.

AROUND CROYDON

1 Diversity
Rachel Stevens
Dingwall Road
Croydon BID

2 Circuit Bus
Eloise Kerr
Dingwall Road
Transport for London

3 Crystal
Sophie Green
The Whitgift Shopping Centre
The Whitgift Shopping Centre

4 Moquette
Design: Mini Moderns.
Created by Michele Pouncey.
The Whitgift Shopping Centre
The Whitgift Shopping Centre

5 Flower Fairies
Michelle Heron
The Whitgift Shopping Centre
The Whitgift Shopping Centre

6 Poppy the Party Bus
Jenny Leonard
North End
Centrale Shopping Centre

7 The '75' to Crocus Valley
Lis Watkins
Saffron Square
Berkeley Homes

8 Wild Ride
Jennie Grover
Wandle Park
Year of the Bus

9 Queen of the Sky
Deven Bhurke
Church Street
Year of the Bus

10 Do The Locomotive
Anna Rawles and
Jennifer Rodgers
Reeves Corner
Year of the Bus

11 Trammin'
Alice Cretney
Charles Street
Berkeley Homes

12 Surrey Street Market
Matt Bannister
Matthew's Yard
Year of the Bus

13 The Library
Anna Rawles and
Jennifer Rodgers
Katharine Street
Year of the Bus

14 Croydon Layers
Matt Bannister
Mint Walk
London Borough of Croydon

15 At The Bottom of The Garden
Anna Benson
The Queen's Gardens
Year of the Bus

16 Magic Bus – Magic Carpet
Giles Boardman
Fairfield Gardens
Year of the Bus

17 Pearl
Janet Fishwick
College Road
Year of the Bus

'Wild Ride' had a wildlife theme and was sited in Wandle Park.

All of the sculpture buses (except the one given an extended stay outside Westminster City Hall) were brought together at the Olympic Park at Stratford on the weekend of 24th and 25th January 2015 for a family event. LT312, following its time in Dundee, was also on show as were the two new sculpture buses needed to bring the total up to 60. In the run up to the event, the 59th bus was painted into a simple leaf design with shrubbery on the roof. Shown in the weekend's programme as 'Jungle Bus', the artist preferred the name 'Rootmaster'. The last one, Icon Bus, is seen opposite being completed by three artists on the Sunday. The third photo on this page shows visitors taking advantage of the 'blackboard' areas of the Accessibus to write ideas or their name on it in chalk.

Special Service
LTZ 1312
Victoria 38
Discover it

60 YEARS
2014

BORIS MOVES ON

Boris Johnson's decision, announced in August 2014, not to stand as mayor of London in 2016 and instead pursue ambitions in parliament, was followed two months later by a TfL decision to buy another 200 New Routemasters. Financial approval for this was requested and granted at TfL's Finance and Policy Committee meeting at Palestra House on 14th October. The Board subsequently gave the formal go-ahead for the order on 5th November. The figure of 200 was not calculated with regard to any specific need but was the number that Wrightbus was expected to be able to complete sometime in 2016. In fact it was stated (perhaps optimistically) that all would be delivered by April 2016.

Either all or the great majority of the 200 extra buses ordered in November 2014, for 100% one-person operation, would be very similar to the Euro VI LTs. The rear door design was being updated; the curved part of the rear doors on the first batch would become a fixed glass panel on the new buses and the rear doors would be plug type like the centre ones. Full air conditioning was ruled out, but modifications to the air cooling system were to be made, with better insulation around areas such as the engine compartment and improved ventilation. Variants on the design were still being considered at this time and some alternative specification buses might be included within the 200. In fact it seemed likely that a small batch of two-door versions would be built. Some further details were also made available of routes surveyed for New Routemasters, which for the first time listed those that were unsuitable for the LT 'without undertaking varying degrees of infrastructure work'. These routes were 7, 14, 19, 22, 23, 74, 94, 139, 168, 414 and C2. Routes surveyed and found to be suitable included the 12, 15, 55, 56, 73, 88, 137, 159, 189, 205 and 453.

One bus from the Euro VI batch destined for the 453, LT299, had visited Edinburgh for a bus garage open day on 27th September. It displayed the weight 12180kgs, but this proved to be incorrect and vehicles of the 453 batch actually weighed 12430kgs with a legal capacity of 81 (to achieve the capacity of 87 legally, the buses would need to weigh no more than 12016kgs). However, with Euro VI technology being heavier, other types on London service were also above this target maximum weight by now. LT299 went straight to Edinburgh from Ballymena and then completed its journey to London. Another bus, LT297, went to a NATO conference in Newport, South Wales, on 4th September.

LT279 in Whitehall on its first day in service. Earlier in the year TfL were looking at the possibility of having the latest technology in digital displays for destination indicators to recreate the look of a destination blind and reduce weight. Euro VI LTs have one small visible external difference from the Euro V buses – a stainless steel scoop over the exhaust at the rear.

The first of the production batch of Euro VI New Routemasters (LTs 273 to 311) entered service on route 453 from Go-Ahead's Mandela Way garage on 18th October, the same weekend that the Sculpture Bus Trail appeared in London. The introduction of New Routemasters on the route was intended to be completed by mid-November but this actually occurred in mid-December as there were delays with commissioning some of the vehicles.

The Euro VI engines for the LTs are built at the Cummins factory in Shanghai rather than Darlington. The latter factory now concentrates on 6-cylinder engines and Shanghai on 4-cylinder ones, the latter having a high demand across Asia. Engines from both factories performed well, according to engineers on the ground, but issues with the batteries meant they were working longer and harder and needed more frequent oil changes and shorter maintenance cycles than other buses. There is a specified 28-day maintenance cycle on the LTs compared with 35 days on other types. To maintain their prestigious appearance, New Routemasters are also cleaned more frequently. A full interior clean is done two or three days a week compared with once a week on other buses. The grooved Treadmaster flooring and stairs are among the areas needing more attention.

On the routes that were staffed with CAs, some of the original conductors had left by now and new recruits were given on-the-job training by an experienced CA over a period of one week. Once all the basics had been demonstrated, the trainer sat next to the rear platform to alert the trainee to hazards that might be being overlooked and to point out places of interest.

All-over adverts continued to appear, with two of the Mandela Way LTs (275 and 294) being for Ugg boots. A third vehicle, LT282, ran in all white. At other garages, a new all-over advert appeared – this time for software producer Android – which continued the trend for new adverts to be white-based. Another special livery was applied to Stockwell's LT60 – another reference to the anniversary of the RM. The bus was taken out of service on 29th October to be painted in a truly splendid LGOC livery, re-entering service in mid-November. By happy coincidence, LT60 was with the present-day London General company.

The black and white of it. Latterly, some of the Adidas LTs ran in all black, while one LT entered service in all-over white, in which it remained for some months, possibly as a result of a cancelled advert.

LT60 was painted by ADL Harlow in this very attractive General livery, including a gold General fleetname on the rear roof dome. It was at first fitted with Year of the Bus branding but this was soon replaced by a gold roundel. At the time it entered service in this livery, LT60 was expected to keep it until 2018 at least.

Brixton garage received LTs 317 to 356 for the 137, six or seven more than was needed for the 30 pvr route plus spares; this was due to the late switch of the buses that had been earmarked for the 159. LT340 is seen a Hyde Park Corner, where the route met New Routemasters on routes 9, 10 and 38. The 73 would be joining them in 2015.

It had been planned that the next route after the 453 would be one of the last (if not the last) to be introduced with customer assistants. Route 159 was the route selected (a nice choice in view of its role as the last Routemaster route) with conductor operation planned between Marble Arch and Brixton Garage. However, the route was lost by Arriva at tender review and the plan changed. Arriva's route 137 was chosen instead and training of conductors was scheduled to start on 13th October for a planned 15th November start. However, Arriva was told by TfL to call off the training programme shortly before it began: the 137 was now going to be opo (as was the 159 when it eventually converted). LTs for the 137 began to arrive on 13th November and the first entered service on the 137 on 2nd December with a target for completion of the end of the year. The route was fully LT-operated by Christmas. The buses for this route saw a temporary reversion to Euro V specification and also had some special Arriva features that meant the six or seven surplus vehicles were not suitable for transfer to the next route to be converted, the 55/N55 in January 2015. They were retained by Arriva until the conversion of the 73 later in the year, planned – at the end of 2014 – to be the last to be introduced with conductors. In the event it was converted to LT without them.

By now the future of the bus had moved some way from Boris's vision of 600 hop-on, hop-off buses. The legacy of a pleasing addition to bus design remains and, had Wrightbus been given an extra year or so to develop the vehicle, the problems of its first few years of service may have been avoided. Its technical template includes the flexibility to accommodate other forms of power, including wireless charging, one of the features giving scope for further development of the design.

Above right: All-over liveried Poppy buses for the annual Poppy Appeal first appeared in 2013. The first New Routemaster with this livery was LT269 in 2014. The bus is seen in Bow.

Right: The occasional special running days along parts or all of long established London bus routes give opportunities for the New Routemaster to be photographed in service alongside its classic predecessors; 2014 was the 75th anniversary of RT1 entering service. The 75th anniversary of LT1 entering service will be 2087. What will preserved examples of these be running alongside?

Tottenham Court Road
8
Stagecoach
In Flanders fields the poppies blow
LTZ 1269

Liverpool Street
11
LTZ 1043
Haig
in
every
LOCAL
HOTEL
HOME
HAMMERSMITH
FULHAM BROADWAY
CHELSEA VICTORIA
CHARING CROSS BANK
11
ALDWYCH
OLD 566

Above left: One of the liveries proposed but not used for the 2014 Year of the Bus was a Shillibeer colour scheme. It would have been a much modernised version, but here Keith McGillivray shows how a livery closer to the scheme applied to a number of Routemasters and a DMS in 1979 might have looked. He shows it on a route that runs along part of Shillibeer's original horse drawn service.

Above: The time when London Transport operated the express Green Line services are acknowledged in this fantasy drawing of a New Routemaster on one of these routes. The Green Line livery was particularly attractive when applied to a double-deck vehicle and would certainly suit this design.

ILLUSTRATION CREDITS

Don Akrigg 154 top, 155 top
Alexander Dennis Ltd 38
Chris Ashby 24 top
Back Boris Campaign 7
Justin Bailey 135 top, 136 top
Ian Banks 167 top
Peter Barclay Inside front cover top, 129 bottom
David Bell 71
Louis Berk 4 lower
Terry Blackman 72, 73, 89 top, 93
Blake Cotterill Design 19 bottom
Gavin Booth, 60, 61, 62, 63, 64, 178 bottom
British Model Buses 95 top
Bus Interchange (businterchange.net) 103
Capoco Design 9, 10, 36, 37
Simon Clark 147 top
Concrete All Round Creative and TfL 26 bottom
Jason Cross 133
Evening Standard 83
Foreign & Commonwealth Office 99, 100, 101, 104, 105
Fran Cush 30
Chang Kin Wai 103, 106, 107, 108
Nigel Eadon-Clarke 88
Peter Edgar 171 top
Ivan Frontani, based in drawings copyright TfL 39
Martin Ford 167 bottom
Foster + Partners and TfL 11, 34, 35
Richard Godfrey 94
Nick Green 181 top
Phil Halewood 132, 134 bottom
Daniel Hardcastle 95 lower centre
Haymarket Media Group Ltd 65, 76, 77, 78, 79, 80, 81
Angela Healey 177 top
Hilton Holloway and Lineale Design 25
Hilton Holloway 55, 57, 58
Hong Yeo 20
Peter Horrex 205 top
Ji Hun Lee 21, 22, 23
Gordon Low 156, 157
Mark Lyons 139 lower
Ian Jordan 68, 97 lower
Mark Kehoe Front cover, 43, 44, 45, 46, 47, 48, 49 bottom, 96, 123, 140 top, 203, 207 bottom
Keith McGillivray Back cover, 50, 92, 134 top, 158, 159, 164 bottom right, 165 centre, 165 bottom, 173, 175 bottom, 202
Jamie Martin 13 bottom
Alan Millar 67, 86, 113, 114, 115, 172
Model Bus Zone 95 bottom
Raj Nahal 17
Ray Parnaby 129 top, 138, 205 bottom
Sergei Polomskikh 32
Pope Wainwright 16
Press Association 3, 13 top, 98, 126
Ogle Noor 27
Jukka Rautiainen 19 top
Reiko Ito, Japan 18
Kim Rennie 128, 170 top, 204 bottom, 207 top
Andrew Riley 116 top
Ian Rivett 166 top
Doug Rose (dougrose.co.uk) 4 upper, 5 upper
Joshua Sharp 155 bottom
Jimmy Sheng 116 bottom
Kevin Smith 82, 84, 120, 124
Malcolm Soh 111
Srokowski Design Ltd 185 top, 185 centre
Colin Stannard 169 top left
Suntec City, Singapore 109, 110
Tata Elxsi 26 top
TfL 142-145
TfL Press Office 41
Times Newspapers Ltd 118/119
Toby Tinsley 14, 15
Philip Wallis 149 bottom
David Warren 135 bottom, 147 bottom, 153, 160, 161 bottom, 164 centre
Rob Wilson 187 centre
Wrightbus Ltd 102
Russell Young 69 bottom left, 164 top, 164 bottom left, 168 top left, 170 bottom
Peter Zabek 90/91, 139 top, 148 top, 162, 163

Photographs not otherwise credited are copyright Capital Transport Publishing Ltd